MYSTERIOUS DEATHS

Marilyn Monroe

by Adam Woog

Lucent Books
P.O. Box 289011, San Diego, CA 92198-9011

These and other titles are included in the *Mysterious Deaths* series:

Butch Cassidy	The Little Princes in the Tower
Amelia Earhart	Malcolm X
John F. Kennedy	Marilyn Monroe
Abraham Lincoln	Mozart

Cover design: Carl Franzen

Library of Congress Cataloging-in-Publication Data

Woog, Adam, 1953-
    Marilyn Monroe / by Adam Woog
        p. cm.—(Mysterious Deaths)
    Includes bibliographical references and index.
    ISBN 1-56006-265-7 (alk. paper)
    1. Monroe, Marilyn, 1926–1962—Death and burial.   I. Title.
II. Series.
PN2287.M69W67   1997
791.43'028'092—dc20   96–22300
    [B]   CIP

Printed in the U.S.A.
Copyright © 1997 by Lucent Books, Inc.
P.O. Box 289011, San Diego, CA 92198-9011

Contents

Haunting Human History

The *Mysterious Deaths* series focuses on nine individuals whose deaths have never been fully explained. Some are figures from the distant past; others are far more contemporary. Yet all of them remain fascinating as much for who they were and how they lived as for how they died. Their lives were characterized by fame and fortune, tragedy and triumph, secrets that led to acute vulnerability. Our enduring fascination with these stories, then, is due in part to the lives of the victims and in part to the array of conflicting facts and opinions, as well as the suspense, that surrounds their deaths.

Some of the people profiled in the *Mysterious Deaths* series were controversial political figures who lived and died in the public eye. John F. Kennedy, Abraham Lincoln, and Malcolm X were all killed in front of crowds as guards paid to protect them were unable to stop their murders. Despite all precautions, their assassins found ample opportunity to carry out their crimes. In each case, the assassins were tried and convicted. So what remains mysterious? As the reader will discover, everything.

The two women in the series, Marilyn Monroe and Amelia Earhart, are equally well remembered. Both died at the heights of their careers; both, from all appearances, had everything to live for. Yet their deaths have also been shrouded in mystery. While there are simple explanations—Monroe committed suicide, Earhart's plane crashed—the public has never been able to accept them. The more researchers dig into the deaths, the more mysterious evidence they unearth. Monroe's predilection for affairs with prominent politicians may have led to her death. Earhart, brash and cavalier, may have been involved in a government plot that collapsed around her. And these theories do not exhaust the mysterious possibilities that continue to puzzle researchers.

The circumstances of the deaths of the remaining figures in the *Mysterious Deaths* series—Richard III's nephews Edward and

Richard; the brilliant composer Wolfgang Mozart; and the infamous bank robber Butch Cassidy—are less well known but no less fascinating.

For example, what are almost surely the skeletons of the little princes Edward and Richard were found buried at the foot of a stairway in the Tower of London in 1674. To many, the discovery proved beyond a doubt that their evil uncle, Richard III, murdered them to attain the throne. Yet others find Richard wrongly accused, the obvious scapegoat. The mysterious tale of their deaths—full of dungeons, plots, and treachery—is still intriguing today.

In the history books, Wolfgang Mozart died in poverty from a consumptive-like disease. Yet there are reports and rumors, snatches of information culled from distant records, that Mozart may have died from a slow poisoning. Who could have wanted to murder the famous composer? And why?

Finally, bank robber Butch Cassidy's death couldn't have been less mysterious—shot to death by military police in Bolivia along with his companion, the Sundance Kid. Then why did members of Butch Cassidy's family and numerous others swear to have seen him, in full health, in the United States years after his supposed death?

These true-life whodunits are filled with tantalizing "what ifs?" What if Kennedy had used the bulletproof plastic hood that his Secret Servicemen had ready? What if Lincoln had decided not to attend the theater—which he did only to please his wife? What if Monroe's friend, Peter Lawford, receiving no answer to his persistent calls, had gone to her house, as he wanted to do? These questions frustrate us as well as testify to a haunting aspect of human history—the way that seemingly insignificant decisions can alter its course.

 *The Screen Goddess*

To put it briefly, she had a quality no one else ever had on the screen except Garbo. No one.

director Billy Wilder

It's nice to be included in people's fantasies, but you also like to be accepted for your own sake. . . . In a way I'm a very unfortunate woman. All this nonsense about being a legend, all this glamour and publicity. Somehow I'm always a disappointment to people.

Marilyn Monroe

At the peak of her career, Marilyn Monroe was the most famous movie star in the world. People around the world knew her as a larger-than-life symbol of Hollywood glamour and sex appeal. On the surface, she seemed to have it all: money; fame; the love of adoring fans; and the attention of powerful, handsome men. Yet this glamorous life was also heartbreakingly sad, cut short by a mysterious and tragic death.

Marilyn's mother, Gladys Monroe Baker, was a flapper—a term used to define a woman in the 1920s who liked both alcohol (which was illegal at the time) and the nonstop partying that often went with it. Her idol was Jean Harlow, the wisecracking blond movie star, and Gladys dreamed of stardom herself. In fact, she consoled herself with the idea that her dull job in a factory that spliced filmstrips together was at least in the movie industry.

In 1919 Gladys briefly married a man named Baker, the father of her first daughter, Berniece. She left Baker for a man named Edward Mortensen, and after separating from him became pregnant again. Norma Jean Mortensen was born on June 1, 1926, at Los Angeles County Hospital. Although the birth certificate lists Mortensen, address unknown, as the father, Gladys was never sure who Norma Jean's real father was and changed Norma's name to Baker.

Gladys was unable or unwilling to care for the new baby. As Marilyn herself put it years later, "My mother didn't want me. I proba-

At her peak, Marilyn Monroe was synonymous with glamour, beauty, and a type of tragic fragility that people still find fascinating today.

bly got in her way, and I must have been a disgrace to her." At the same time, she was unwilling to put the baby up for permanent adoption. Within two weeks of her birth, Norma Jean was sent to live with a foster family, where she spent the first seven years of her life. Albert and Ida Bolender were a strict, religious couple who had one son and an ever-changing parade of foster kids. Their severe beliefs included the conviction that any form of praise led to the sin of vanity. Their foster children were never hugged, never told that they did well, never given undue amounts of attention. No matter how hard young Norma Jean tried to perform a given task, her work was never good enough for her foster parents.

Norma Jean's early years were lonely. She never became close to the Bolenders or the other foster children. Her closest companion was Tippy, a dog the Bolenders gave her. Her mother's visits were occasional and sporadic.

Marilyn as a toddler. Her mother's erratic behavior and alcoholism marred her childhood and adolescence.

An Arranged Marriage

This restricted life suddenly changed in 1933 when Gladys impulsively decided to take Norma Jean back. The young girl abruptly went from the strict life of the Bolenders' house to Gladys's carefree home, which she shared with her best friend, Grace McKee. Gladys drank beer, smoked cigarettes, played cards, stayed up late, and gossiped about the movies.

Unfortunately, Gladys's heavy drinking, combined with drugs given to her by a physician to fight depression, led to increasingly erratic behavior such as crying jags, drinking binges, and shouting matches. The next year, at age thirty-one, Gladys was sent to a hospital for alcoholics. She was diagnosed as mentally ill and spent virtually the rest of her life in various institutions, unable to care for herself or for her daughter.

Grace McKee became Norma Jean's legal guardian. She loved Norma Jean and gave her the steadiest, most substantial support the girl had ever received. However, shortly after Grace became the girl's guardian in 1935, she married a man who didn't want children. For several years Norma Jean was shuttled between an orphanage and the homes of various relatives. To compensate for the instability of her young life, Norma Jean took refuge in a world of make-believe; as she remarked later, "The world around me then was kind of grim. I had to learn to pretend in order to . . . block the grimness."

In school, Norma Jean was quiet and shy. She dressed in cheap sandals and ill-fitting dresses. She had a slight stutter and no close friends. Other kids teased her with nicknames like "the Mouse" and "Norma Jean the String Bean."

The nicknames ended, though, when her figure started to fill out in the eighth grade. Norma Jean had always had a beautiful, fresh face and a wonderful smile—but suddenly the string bean was becoming very popular with the boys. Eventually, Norma Jean would learn that the world could be cruel and shallow; although men would always desire her body, Norma would always be insecure, knowing that her beauty was a superficial thing to be loved for. All her life, she would search for someone who could accept her for herself, her intelligence, curiosity, and drive. This struggle was ultimately unsuccessful, and it left her with what biographer Fred Lawrence Guiles called "a sense of worthlessness that no amount of love and reassurance could overcome."

"Every Current of Rumor"

In Marilyn: A Biography, *novelist Norman Mailer summarizes the many theories surrounding Monroe's death.*

"Just as the trail of Jack Kennedy's assassination in Dallas may be lost forever in the tracks of a thousand terrified moves by people who crossed over that trail in fear others were implicated, so too will her death be confused by every current of rumor until it is not possible to decide if she was dead of a suicide by barbiturates (after all the ones that failed), or by the accident of taking, as she had on many another night, more barbiturates than she could carefully count, or whether she was even— . . . murdered, . . . and if that is the wildest of suppositions, with the feeblest of evidence to support it, there was motive nonetheless for murder and no weak motive."

A major change in Norma Jean's life occurred while she was still in high school. Grace moved away from Los Angeles, and the only relative who might have taken Norma Jean in, her Aunt Ana, was seriously ill. For Norma Jean, still a minor, there was only one option beyond the orphanage: to get married.

Grace decided that marriage was the best plan for Norma Jean. She arranged with the parents of a handsome young man, Jim Dougherty, for the pair to marry. Jim, a few years older than Norma Jean and already employed at the Lockheed aircraft plant, knew her casually and agreed to the match. A few days after her sixteenth birthday, Norma Jean quit the tenth grade and married Jim Dougherty.

At sixteen, Marilyn married Jim Dougherty. As could be expected, the marriage lasted only two years.

Marilyn started modeling when she was "discovered" by a photographer at the defense plant where she worked during World War II. She went on to a successful modeling career, as this sample of her early work can attest.

Modeling and Movies

By this time America had entered the Second World War. When Dougherty was drafted and sent overseas, Norma Jean got a job in a defense plant. It was in this unlikely place that she began her professional career.

The star-to-be was discovered when a group of photographers came to the plant to document the role of women in the war effort. One of these men, a commercial photographer named David Conover, was particularly struck by Norma Jean; he thought she had modeling potential and urged her to pursue this goal. In her spare time, she started posing for him, mostly for brochures and other material related to the war effort and the defense industry.

By the war's end in 1945, Norma Jean was on the road to a successful modeling career. She signed up with a prestigious modeling

agency and dyed her hair blond. She was appearing on dozens of
magazine covers and advertisements, and she was earning good
money. There were also nibbles from the movie industry.

From the beginning, she showed a strong drive to overcome her
humble origins. As the modeling agency's director recalled, "She
started out with less than any girl I ever knew, but she worked the
hardest." Unfortunately, her husband did not share her ambition.
Dougherty, back from the war, wanted his wife to quit modeling.
She refused and their relationship became strained. In 1946 she
filed for divorce.

That summer Norma Jean signed a six-month contract with one
of Hollywood's biggest movie studios, 20th Century-Fox. As one of
dozens of young hopefuls signed to low-paying studio contracts,
she earned seventy-five dollars a week "on contract"; that is, she
was paid whether she worked or not. Contract starlets were required to appear in whatever films were being shot at the time. A
tiny handful of starlets would eventually move up the ranks and
become genuine stars.

"Marilyn Monroe" was born at Fox when the studio executives
decided that the name Norma Jean Baker wasn't glamorous
enough. A casting director chose the name Marilyn because

Norma Jean reminded him of actress Marilyn Miller. Her surname, Monroe, was her mother's maiden name.

Marilyn's movie career began slowly. Her first role had only one speaking line. Other equally obscure roles followed. When her contract ended, Monroe took odd jobs and studied acting. Money was scarce; later, Monroe admitted that during this period she was forced into occasional prostitution in order to make ends meet.

Stardom and Marriage

Marilyn finally got a lucky break when she met a string of influential men, including Joseph Schenck, an executive at Fox; Harry Cohn, the head of Columbia Studios; and Johnny Hyde, an important agent. She had affairs with all three, and all three helped her career. For the rest of her life, Monroe was attracted to powerful, older men; she remained unable to escape the close connection between sexual favors and success.

Better movie roles came along, including small but juicy roles in two popular films, *The Asphalt Jungle* and *All About Eve*. She also continued to model, became *Playboy* magazine's first centerfold, and signed a long-term contract with Fox in 1951.

By the mid-fifties Monroe was a star, thanks to a series of high-profile roles in such films as *Don't Bother to Knock, Monkey Business, Niagara, Gentlemen Prefer Blondes,* and *How to Marry a Millionaire*. She should have been making a great deal of money, but her contract with Fox was less than generous.

Meanwhile, Monroe met the love of her life. When he met Monroe in 1952, the legendary baseball slugger Joe DiMaggio was already an American hero and a man with a permanent place in baseball history. The starlet was twenty-five; "Joltin' Joe" was thirty-seven, divorced, and retired from a long and brilliant career with the New York Yankees. Monroe was attracted to DiMaggio's tall, athletic presence and graceful, reserved manner. He also treated Monroe decently—a rarity among the men she knew. The attraction was mutual, and gossip columns soon began speculating about "the slugger and the starlet."

They were wed in 1954, but the marriage was stormy from the beginning. DiMaggio enjoyed the privileges of fame but hated crowds and glamour. He liked to stay home and watch sports on TV. Monroe, on the other hand, craved parties, bright lights, and good conversation. DiMaggio came from a deeply conservative Italian-

Marilyn in a still for the movie Gentlemen Prefer Blondes. *Monroe was able to break into movies by fostering relationships with powerful men.*

American family; he was offended that his new wife enjoyed showing off her sexiness in the movies or in public. As he once remarked sourly to a reporter, "It's not easy being married to an electric light."

The situation deteriorated quickly. At home, DiMaggio was moody; he sometimes did not speak to Marilyn for a week at a time. If she questioned him and tried to find out what was wrong, he complained about her nagging. There were reports that DiMaggio insulted Monroe in public. There were even rumors that he sometimes physically abused her. After only nine months of marriage, Monroe filed for divorce.

New York, London, Another Marriage, Pills

Her second divorce was another tragedy for a woman who had led a rough life and was already sensitive to failure. She had desperately wanted her marriage to work, and it had not. Marilyn decided to start her life over by leaving her familiar surroundings; in early 1955 she moved to New York for what would be a year-long vacation.

She led a quiet life in New York. Her daily routine revolved around two main activities: acting lessons with Lee Strasberg, the founder of an influential dramatic technique called the Method

School, and daily sessions of psychoanalysis with a Freudian analyst, Dr. Marilyn Hohenberg. Beyond these activities, Monroe saw only a few friends and spent much of her time sorting out the details of an independent production company she wanted to form with a photographer friend, Milton Greene.

A new man also entered her life: Arthur Miller. The athletic, intellectual Miller was the author of *Death of a Salesman, The Crucible*, and many other highly regarded plays; he was considered one of the most respected playwrights in America. His own marriage was failing, and he soon became Monroe's regular companion despite the age difference: at thirty-nine he was a decade older than Monroe. As DiMaggio had been, Miller was swept away by her presence. "It was wonderful to be around her," he recalled later. "She was simply overwhelming. She had so much promise."

By the spring of 1956, Monroe was ready to return to moviemaking. Her longtime makeup artist and friend, Allan (Whitey) Snyder,

Marilyn wed baseball star Joe DiMaggio in 1954. Although they would later divorce, he remained loyal to her until her death.

Marilyn wed playwright Arthur Miller in 1956. The marriage would be troubled from the start.

later recalled that she appeared revitalized: "She seemed content and more serious than before." Monroe's first film after her break was *Bus Stop*, a drama that was a success with both critics and fans.

She and Miller were married and went to England so that she could film a comedy, *The Prince and the Showgirl*. Unfortunately, both the shooting and the new marriage soon turned sour.

The film's costar and director, Sir Laurence Olivier, openly disliked Monroe—he hated her insecurities and sloppy, unprofessional conduct—and went out of his way to humiliate her. Olivier's wife, actress Vivien Leigh, also publicly made fun of what she considered Monroe's small ability. The humiliations weakened Monroe's already fragile sense of self-esteem.

Even more devastating was Monroe's discovery of Miller's diary, in which he admitted to having second thoughts about his new wife, calling her "unpredictable," "forlorn," and "immature." This led to tearful shouting matches and stony silences between the newlyweds. The trip's final disaster came when Monroe, who desperately wanted children, suffered a miscarriage.

Monroe was having other problems as well. She had always suffered from insomnia, the inability to sleep. She used curtains to block light from her bedroom as well as earplugs and a sleeping mask; even so, it was always hard for her to sleep. Her insomnia, coupled with a busy schedule, meant that Monroe was always on the verge of exhaustion.

To help her, Hollywood psychiatrist Dr. Ralph Greenson regularly prescribed heavy doses of sleeping pills. The use of sleeping pills was not an unusual thing at the time, especially among show business people and other celebrities. The effects of their long-term use were not yet fully understood, and doctors often gave them out freely. By the mid-fifties, Monroe was addicted to them.

Downhill Slide

Following her return to New York after finishing the movie with Olivier, Monroe's life continued to go badly. Her new husband, for one thing, was depressed over a serious case of writer's block; he

Real Beauty

In an interview for LIFE *magazine shortly before her death and reprinted in Spoto's* Marilyn Monroe: The Biography, *Monroe frankly shared some of her thoughts.*

"What goes with it [fame] can be a burden. Real beauty and femininity are ageless and can't be contrived. Glamour can be manufactured. Fame is certainly only a cause for temporary and partial happiness—not for a daily diet, it's not what fulfills you. It warms you a bit, but the warming is only temporary. When you're famous every weakness is exaggerated. Fame will go by and—so long, fame, I've had you! I've always known it was fickle. It was something I experienced, but it's not where I live.

Successful, happy and on time—those are all the glib American clichés. I don't want to be late, but I usually am, much to my regret. Often, I'm late because I'm preparing a scene, maybe preparing too much sometimes. But I've always felt that even in the slightest scene the people ought to get their money's worth. And this is an obligation of mine, to give them the best. When they go to see me and look up at the screen, they don't know I was late. And by that time, the studio has forgotten all about it and is making money."

had been working on a screenplay based on his short story about modern-day cowboys, "The Misfits," but was having difficulty completing it; to make matters worse, his income was low during this period, and Monroe was essentially supporting him.

In addition to her troubled relationship with Miller, Marilyn faced other financial and emotional problems. Her business partner, Milton Greene, had become seriously addicted to prescription drugs; his behavior became increasingly erratic, and eventually she was forced to end their professional relationship. The plans she and Greene had made to form a production company independent from the restraints of Hollywood seemed doomed. Finally, she kept trying to have children but suffered another miscarriage.

There were a few bright spots in Marilyn's life, including a new psychiatrist, Dr. Marianne Kris, whom she liked immensely. Also, in 1959 Monroe shot *Some Like It Hot*, a comedy that many consider to be her finest work.

Worsening Habits

During the shooting of *Some Like It Hot*, Monroe's work habits, which had always been sloppy, worsened. She would fuss for hours over proposed makeup or costume changes as the others involved in production waited patiently. She would take a dislike to a particular dress, or she would be unhappy with her looks, or any one of a number of other things might go wrong. As a result, an expensive film crew would be kept waiting. Many around her felt that Monroe's low self-esteem was the main factor in her chronic pattern of indecision and tardiness. The sleeping pills, meanwhile, had locked her into a cycle of drug-induced sleep at night and a groggy wakefulness during the day. The drugs affected her work on the set. Dozens of retakes were necessary for each scene, because she had problems remembering even the simplest lines.

On the other hand, when Monroe was "on"—when her creative light was shining—she was brilliant. She had a luminous quality that made her presence unique—and that compensated, at least in part, for her deficiencies. As Billy Wilder, the director of *Some Like It Hot*, put it, "Anyone can remember lines, but it takes a real artist to come on the set and *not* know her lines and yet give the performance she did!"

Marilyn Monroe poses with costars Clark Gable (right) and Montgomery Clift (left) in a publicity still for the movie The Misfits. *It was the last film for Monroe and Gable.*

Some Like It Hot was followed by another comedy, *Let's Make Love*, and then by Miller's modern western, *The Misfits*, in which his wife had a leading role. It was the last film she would complete.

The final version is a fine movie, but the shooting of *The Misfits* in Nevada was a complete disaster. Everything seemed to go wrong despite the star power attached to the project; the film also involved the legendary director John Huston and three excellent actors: Clark Gable, Eli Wallach, and Montgomery Clift.

During the filming, Miller and Monroe had separate hotel suites, were barely speaking, and were headed toward divorce. The aging but still athletic Gable insisted on doing his own dangerous

Monroe's psychiatrist Ralph Greenson may have fostered an inappropriately dependent relationship with Monroe.

stunts and was egged on by the macho director Huston. The stunts may have been Gable's undoing; a few weeks after the film was completed, he suffered a fatal heart attack.

Huston, meanwhile, was drinking heavily and gambling all night. The final blow to the film's production came when Huston gambled away fifty thousand dollars of the movie's budget. When the studio threatened to shut down production, Huston managed to convince company executives that Monroe had a serious barbiturate problem and needed a week of rest in a private hospital. This break gave the director time to cover the debt from other sources. The news spread that Monroe had suffered a nervous breakdown. This rumor was not true, although she was in very fragile condition; however, on the advice of her psychiatrist, she did take time off, giving Huston the time he needed.

Monroe filed for divorce in early 1961 and settled again in Los Angeles. Monroe's primary psychiatrist, Ralph Greenson, began playing an even larger role in her life.

Greenson had a strange relationship with Monroe. His patients included many celebrities, and as a psychiatrist he was required to maintain an emotional distance from them, but he was infatuated with Monroe. He openly bragged about his famous patient, revealed her secrets to colleagues, and introduced her to his family, all actions which are serious breaches of professional ethics. At various times he even moved her into the house he shared with his wife and children, explaining that Monroe was not able to be separated from him.

At the same time, Greenson was condescending and controlling, often treating Monroe like a child. He once wrote in a letter to a colleague that Monroe was "pathetic, such a perpetual orphan." His attitude, in the words of Monroe biographer Donald Spoto, was "more characteristic of a wounded parent or a smug teacher than a sensible counselor committed to the mental health of his patient."

Greenson tried to control his vulnerable client's life in many ways. He persuaded her to fire her friend and masseur, Ralph Roberts, and to stay away from other friends. He also persuaded her to hire a woman named Eunice Murray as a housekeeper-nurse, although Murray, a longtime acquaintance of Greenson's, had no special training for the job. According to many of Monroe's friends, Murray was a spy who reported details of Monroe's actions to Greenson. Pat Newcomb, Monroe's publicist, recalled, "I did not trust Eunice Murray, who seemed to be always snooping around. . . . She was sort of a spook, always hovering, always on the fringe of things."

Also on Greenson's recommendation, Monroe checked into a New York psychiatric hospital after she became seriously depressed over the divorce from Arthur Miller. Apparently by mistake, Monroe was put in a locked and padded cell, and she panicked. "The nuthouse," as the actress called it, unleashed in her a deep-rooted fear of insanity, and it brought back painful memories of her mentally unstable mother.

After two terrifying days in her locked room, Monroe was finally allowed one phone call. She called Joe DiMaggio.

Return to Hollywood

Despite their divorce, Joe and Marilyn had remained close friends. Their personality differences and inability to live together had not altered their affection for each other. Now, when she needed him, DiMaggio came immediately to her rescue. He flew to New York from his home in Florida, arranged for her release, and took her home with him. During this period of convalescence, the romance was rekindled.

That summer she returned to Los Angeles and bought a small, Spanish-style house close to Greenson's home. The address was 12305 Fifth Helena Drive; the street's unusual name results from its being one of several dead-end streets known as "the numbered Helenas." She also began work on *Something's Got to Give*, a comedy costarring Dean Martin. This uncompleted project would be her final film.

The filming, which took place during the last weeks of Monroe's life, was yet another disaster. Monroe's notorious problems on the set, coupled with a sinus infection that forced her to take frequent days off, threatened to send the picture far over budget. The Fox

Marilyn Monroe sings "Happy Birthday" to President John F. Kennedy in Madison Square Garden in 1962. The appearance fostered rumors about the pair.

studio was in serious financial trouble and its executives were desperate to stop further losses. When they finally decided to fire her, Monroe's costar Dean Martin, loyal to his friend, walked off the set. Fox was forced to rehire her and negotiate a settlement.

At the End

During these final weeks, Monroe seemed in some ways to be trying to reclaim her runaway life. She was recognizing that she needed to establish some stability, in part by renewing her relationship with DiMaggio. She was beginning to resist Greenson's efforts to isolate her from her friends. She also fired Eunice Murray and wrote the housekeeper a final check, an action that angered both Murray and Greenson.

Then Monroe disrupted filming again by flying to New York for President John F. Kennedy's birthday party. The event, a Democratic Party fund-raiser at Madison Square Garden, featured a long list of celebrity performers. Monroe, who was active in Democratic politics and knew both President Kennedy and his brother, Attorney General Robert F. Kennedy, was the show's climax. Dressed in a sequined dress that was so tight she had to be sewn into it, she sang "Happy Birthday" to the president in a breathless, teasingly sexy voice.

When Monroe returned to Los Angeles, Eunice Murray was at the house. Murray, for reasons unknown, decided to regard Monroe's final check as merely a bonus, and she resumed her job as if nothing had happened. Despite Murray's campaign to isolate Monroe, withholding the actress's mail and openly driving her friends away, Monroe was reluctant to fire her again. Finally in early August 1962, Murray announced she was leaving on a European vacation with her sister. Monroe told Murray not to return in the fall.

Shortly before, on a late-July weekend trip to Lake Tahoe, Nevada, Joe and Marilyn had decided to remarry. Susan Strasberg, Monroe's friend and the daughter of her drama coach, believed the marriage was another step in the actress's fight for stability. Strasberg recalled, "She was fighting to take responsibility for her own life, and so she . . . knew she needed some sort of emotional and spiritual anchor."

But even Joe DiMaggio couldn't save Marilyn. By early August, Monroe was dead.

The Death

> Monroe was laughing and chatting on the telephone with Joe DiMaggio's son . . . and not thirty minutes after this happy conversation, *[she] was dying. . . .* This was one of the strangest facts of the case.
>
> from the Los Angeles County Coroner's report

MARILYN, DEAD
> banner headline, August 5, 1962, *Los Angeles Times*

In the summer of 1962, at the age of thirty-six, Marilyn Monroe died in the bedroom of her Los Angeles home. The exact cause of her death—and the reasons behind it—have never been fully determined. Many puzzling details about the incident remain unexplained. According to the official police report, Monroe committed suicide by overdosing on sleeping pills. However, Monroe's death has always held a fascination for researchers, and a number of other theories have emerged over the years.

Some investigators, for instance, think that she killed herself accidentally—that she took too much medication by mistake. Others contend that her longtime psychiatrist, who had grown very close to his famous client, accidentally gave her a drug overdose and then covered up his mistake to make it look like suicide.

There are also theories that contend that Monroe's death was deliberate murder—and that it was part of a complex conspiracy. According to these conjectures, Monroe was romantically involved with either or both President John F. Kennedy and his brother, Attorney General Robert F. Kennedy. Although theories vary in detail, most of them link Monroe and the Kennedys with a variety of people and organizations, including Mafia gangsters, the FBI, labor kingpin Jimmy Hoffa, and entertainers Peter Lawford and Frank Sinatra.

FINAL **DAILY ★ NEWS** **5¢**

NEW YORK'S PICTURE NEWSPAPER®

Vol. 44. No. 36   Copr 1962 News Syndicate Co. Inc.   New York 17, N.Y., Monday, August 6, 1962*   WEATHER: Sunny and humid.

MARILYN DEAD

A headline proclaims Marilyn's tragic death. Ruled suicide by the coroners, the judgment has been questioned ever since.

The Last Day and Night

Marilyn Monroe's last full night alive was the night of Friday, August 3, just five days before her scheduled remarriage to Joe DiMaggio. Monroe and the publicist Pat Newcomb, who worked with her, had a quiet dinner at a local restaurant and returned to Monroe's house. Newcomb had bronchitis, and Monroe invited her to stay overnight and rest by the pool the next day.

The next morning Eunice Murray arrived for her last day of work. Newcomb slept until noon. Murray recalled later that Monroe was annoyed that her friend had been able to sleep so late; Monroe, typically, had been unable to sleep and had awoken early.

25

Peter Lawford and Marilyn Monroe in 1962. Marilyn spent time at the Lawfords' on the day of her death.

Monroe spent the day at home, making plans for the wedding reception, meeting with a photographer about an upcoming magazine article, talking on the phone, and having two psychiatric sessions with Greenson. The psychiatrist arrived around 1:00 P.M. for the first of these sessions. At about 2:00, Joe DiMaggio Jr. (DiMaggio's son from his first marriage) called the house. Stationed with the marines in nearby Orange County, the younger DiMaggio was on friendly terms with Monroe. Although Monroe was in a therapy session with Greenson, Murray lied and told the marine that the actress was not home.

Around 3:00, Greenson emerged from Monroe's bedroom, where he had been conducting the therapy session. Before leaving, he told Newcomb to leave because his patient was upset. He also instructed Murray to take Monroe to actor Peter Lawford's oceanfront house. Greenson wanted Monroe to go for a walk on the beach to calm down. Lawford was Monroe's close friend. He was married to Patricia Kennedy, President Kennedy's sister.

According to witnesses at Lawford's house, Monroe seemed drugged and unsteady when she arrived, and her speech was slurred. Murray left Monroe at Lawford's, went shopping for groceries, and then returned to pick up the actress. They arrived home around 4:30. Joe DiMaggio Jr. called again, and again Murray told him that Monroe was not home. Soon afterwards, Greenson returned for another session with Marilyn.

A Confusion of Calls

Around 5:00, three more close friends phoned Monroe. Peter Lawford wanted her to come back to his house for a casual dinner that evening. Murray told Isadore Miller, Arthur Miller's father, that Monroe was dressing and could not talk. Greenson answered a call from Ralph Roberts and abruptly hung up on the masseur.

Greenson testified later that he left Monroe's house for the second time between 7:00 and 7:15. He had prescribed an extra dose of sedative to help his patient sleep. Before leaving, he asked Murray to stay in the house overnight, which she usually did not do on weekends. Soon after Greenson left, Joe DiMaggio Jr. called again. This time, Monroe answered the phone. According to the marine's testimony later, they spoke for about ten minutes and she seemed alert, happy, and in good spirits.

And yet when Peter Lawford phoned again, around 7:40 or 7:45, still hoping Monroe would come to his house, her manner was dramatically different. Lawford testified that during this call Marilyn was disoriented and that her speech was thick and slurred. She told him, "Say goodbye to Pat [Lawford], say goodbye to the president, and say goodbye to yourself, because you're a nice guy."

One Person

Sometime in the afternoon before her death, Monroe began composing a note to Joe DiMaggio, the man she was soon to remarry. The unfinished note was later found in her address book.

"Dear Joe,

If I can only succeed in making you happy, I will have succeeded in the biggest and most difficult thing there is—that is, to make one person completely happy. Your happiness means my happiness, and   "

Monroe then lapsed into such a long silence that Lawford thought she had hung up. He tried calling again, but got only a busy signal for the next half hour. Worried, he called several other people, all of whom assured him that Monroe would be fine.

Lawford testified later that he had wanted to go to Monroe's house to check on her but that friends convinced him it would be a bad idea. Lawford was in a delicate position; he was the president's brother-in-law, and the repercussions would be serious if a relative of the Kennedy family was caught in an embarrassing situation. What if Lawford went to the house and found Monroe drunk or drugged?

Lawford was by now drinking heavily and becoming increasingly worried. Rather than go to the house himself, he asked a number of other people to go to check on Monroe. Monroe's attorney, Milton Rudin, who was also Greenson's brother-in-law, told Lawford he would phone Eunice Murray. Murray left Rudin waiting on the line for a few minutes and then came back to say that Monroe was fine.

Another friend of Lawford's, producer William Asher, agreed to drop by Monroe's house. Before he could leave his own home, however, he received a phone call from Milton Ebbins, Lawford's friend and the vice president of Lawford's production company. Ebbins told Asher that he had just received a call from Ralph Greenson. The psychiatrist had told Ebbins that he had given Monroe a sedative earlier and that she was resting comfortably. Asher decided to trust the psychiatrist and so did not go to Monroe's house.

Lawford finally gave up trying to get help for Monroe around 1:30 A.M. on Sunday morning. Later that next morning, he got the news that Monroe had died. Milton Ebbins told Lawford that when Ralph Greenson had gone to Monroe's house at midnight, the star was dead.

The Housekeeper's Story

Early on Sunday morning, August 5, Sergeant Jack Clemmons of the Los Angeles Police Department, who was the acting watch commander in charge at the West Los Angeles station, received a shocking phone call. Marilyn Monroe was dead.

Clemmons dashed from the station and arrived at Monroe's house a few minutes later, at 4:35 A.M. Eunice Murray, Ralph Greenson, and Dr. Hyman Engelberg, Monroe's physician, met Clemmons at the door. The story that Murray told Clemmons about the circumstances of the death, a story backed up by Greenson and Engelberg, became the basis for the official investigation. Many investigators, however, have since come to doubt its accuracy.

Murray said that she saw the light on under Monroe's door when she herself went to sleep at 10:00. She assumed the actress was either sleeping or talking on the phone. When Murray got up around midnight to go to the bathroom, she saw that the light was still on and became concerned.

The bedroom door was locked from the inside. Murray knocked but failed to rouse Monroe. She then phoned Greenson, who lived a short distance away. Greenson told Murray to go outside and look through Monroe's bedroom window. The window was open and barred, and the heavy curtains were in place, but Greenson told Murray to part the curtains with a fireplace poker. When she did so, Murray told Clemmons, she saw the actress lying motionless, face down on the bed.

Murray called Greenson again, and he came to the house. When he arrived he went outside and smashed another, unbarred bedroom window with the same fireplace poker. He entered the bedroom and saw that Monroe was dead. Greenson called Engelberg, who also lived in the neighborhood. Engelberg arrived immediately and pronounced the actress dead. It was then, the trio said, that they phoned the police.

Contradictions

The housekeeper's story seemed strange from the beginning. For one thing, Murray said she had noticed that something was wrong around midnight and that she had immediately contacted Greenson and Engelberg. But the phone call to the police had not come until 4:30 in the morning. When Clemmons asked why they had waited so long to notify the police, Greenson replied that they "had to get permission from the publicity department at the studio before we could notify anyone."

Murray must have realized that this excuse sounded flimsy because she later changed her story. By the time a detective interviewed her later that morning, Murray was testifying that she had not woken up and noticed the light under the door of Monroe's room until 3:00 A.M.

Marilyn's room after her death. Puzzling questions remain about the way in which her body was found.

The Death Scene

When Sergeant Clemmons asked to see the body, Murray and the doctors led him to Marilyn's room. The actress was lying face down on the bed with a sheet pulled over her body and a wisp of blond hair sticking out. Her face was buried in a pillow, with her hands by her sides and her legs completely parallel. Clemmons noticed a bluish discoloring of the skin, which typically means that a body has been dead for several hours.

Later investigators emphasized that Monroe was found nude. They find this odd, since she normally slept in a brassiere (to keep her breasts from sagging), along with an eyeshade and earplugs to block out light and sound. This fact has been used to bolster the argument that someone tampered with the body and the scene of Monroe's death.

Clemmons later testified to other strange facts about the death scene. For one thing, he found it unnaturally tidy. He felt that the room had been cleaned up before his arrival. He said later:

The whole place was very neat. . . . The whole part of the house I saw had been picked up. That's not characteristic, because when there's been a suicide, things are usually left lying around the room. Almost nobody is very neat when they are going to commit suicide.

In fact, Murray seemed obsessively interested in cleaning the house. As Clemmons went about his preliminary investigation, Murray kept busy by tidying up. Clemmons could hear the house-keeper running the washing machine and vacuum cleaner in other parts of the house. In some ways this may seem like unusual behavior for someone in a house where tragedy has just struck. On the other hand, therapists who specialize in grief point out that doing mindless busywork is often a common reaction to a shock.

At one point in his investigation, Clemmons asked Greenson how Monroe had killed herself. The psychiatrist pointed to a cluster of bottles, about eight in all, that were on the bedside table. They were all partly empty and at one time had contained portions of various kinds of prescription drugs, mostly sleeping pills. Greenson told Clemmons flatly that Monroe had committed suicide, an opinion he maintained for the rest of his life.

The Mysterious Ambulance

One strange piece of the puzzle of Monroe's last night revolves around an ambulance. Eunice Murray testified, as noted in the district attorney's 1982 report, that Greenson summoned an ambulance around midnight and then dismissed it on arrival—because Monroe was already dead and California law prohibits transporting a corpse in an ambulance.

The district attorney's staff interviewed a former ambulance driver, Ken Hunter, who in 1962 worked for Schaefer Ambulance, the biggest private ambulance company in the Los Angeles area. He said he and another driver were summoned to Monroe's home "in the early morning hours." No press or police had yet reached the scene, nor does he remember any doctors being present.

Walt Schaefer, the president of the ambulance company, confirmed to investigator Anthony Summers that a Schaefer ambulance had been called to Monroe's home. Schaefer said he learned of the call the next morning, and that the bill was later paid by Monroe's estate. But Schaefer also told Summers that—contrary to all the other evidence and testimony—Monroe did not die at home. The ambulance, he said, "took her to Santa Monica Hospital. She passed away at the hospital."

Robert Slatzer, meanwhile, wrote in *The Marilyn Files* that a driver for Schaefer Ambulance, James Hall, claimed to be the atten-

The Body Is Found

In this excerpt from his book The Marilyn Files, *Robert Slatzer—who claims to have been married to Monroe and who thinks she was murdered—describes the death scene.*

"Mrs. Murray and the doctors conducted him [Sgt. Jack Clemmons] to Marilyn's room. Clemmons walked over to the bed. 'Marilyn was lying face down on the bed; a sheet was pulled up over her body, and a wisp of blond hair was sticking out. I didn't want to touch anything while I was there. I didn't even pull the sheet back. I could see she was dead.'

The star's face was buried in a pillow, hands by her sides, her legs completely parallel. Clemmons, who knew that death from drug overdose usually causes convulsions, felt that the body must have been deliberately posed in that position.

Clemmons could also see the typical bluish coloring that indicates postmortem lividity has set in. This confirmed the doctors' story that Marilyn had been dead for several hours by the time the police were notified.

Clemmons asked Dr. Greenson if anyone had moved the body. The physician replied that no one had touched the body beyond ascertaining that the actress was dead. This explanation struck a sour note. Because of the position of the body, Clemmons was convinced it must have been rearranged. Both men were doctors and had the legal right to move the body. If they had moved Marilyn's body, there seemed to be no reason for them to lie about it—unless they were hiding something.

Sergeant Clemmons also saw other signs that the death scene had been rearranged and cleaned up before his arrival. 'The whole place was very neat. The whole part of the house I saw had been picked up. That's not characteristic, because when there's been a suicide, things are usually left lying around the room. Almost nobody is very neat when they are going to commit suicide.'"

A coroner's note seals Marilyn's house on the day of her death. Marilyn's nude body was found face down, a telephone by her side.

dant on the scene. According to Hall, Monroe was in a coma and he began attempts to revive her. These attempts were successful until Ralph Greenson, accompanied by Peter Lawford, arrived at Monroe's house and took over. Hall claimed that the doctor bungled the job, forcing a heart needle into Monroe's chest so carelessly that it snapped off.

As is common with such organizations, the ambulance company and the hospital discarded their records after a certain number of years. There is therefore no way to prove or disprove the existence of the mysterious ambulance or of what may have happened at the hospital. If this story is true, it means that someone called the ambulance, tried to revive Monroe at the hospital, and then—for an unexplained reason—returned her to Fifth Helena in time for Murray and Greenson to call the police at 4:30 A.M.

Who Was There?

According to interviews conducted by Anthony Summers, many people in addition to Greenson, Murray, and Engelberg may have

The Day She Died

Actor Marlon Brando reflects on the shock of Monroe's death, quoted in Ann Lloyd's Marilyn: A Hollywood Life.

"Do you remember when Marilyn Monroe died? Everybody stopped work, and you could see all that day the same expression on their faces, the same thought: How can a girl with success, fame, youth, money, beauty . . . how could she kill herself? Nobody could understand it because those are the things that everybody wants and they can't believe that life wasn't important to Marilyn Monroe, or that her life was elsewhere."

been at Marilyn's home before the police were called. Natalie Jacobs stated that her husband, Monroe's chief publicist Arthur Jacobs, was there within an hour of receiving word of Monroe's death; he got the news at the Hollywood Bowl, where he had been out with friends. This time sequence puts Jacobs at Monroe's house by about 11:30 P.M.

To Anthony Summers, Milt Ebbins corroborated the report that Milton Rudin, Monroe's lawyer, was at her house in the middle of the night. Ebbins stated that the lawyer called him at 4:00 A.M., before the police were called, to say that the actress was dead. According to Summers, Pat Newcomb said during a 1973 interview that she heard news of the death "around four" from Rudin, calling—she thought—from Monroe's home.

No Answer

In 1982, in a statement to the district attorney's staff, Peter Lawford said he was awakened at 1:30 A.M. by a phone call from Ebbins, passing on news from Rudin that Monroe was dead. Lawford said he was sure of the time because he glanced at the bedside clock when Ebbins called. Ebbins, however, has maintained that he did not call Lawford's home until 4:00 A.M. and then got no response. "I called but I couldn't get anyone," Ebbins told Summers. "The phone didn't answer."

Lawford's former wife, Deborah Gould, tells still another story. She told Summers:

Marilyn got on the phone to Peter, grasping out, to inform him that she couldn't take any more, and that it would be best for everybody that she died and she was going to kill herself. Peter had been drinking a great deal and he had a cynical sense of humor, but maybe he didn't take her seriously.

According to Gould, Lawford responded to Marilyn's talk of suicide with, "Nonsense, Marilyn, pull yourself together; but, my God, whatever you do don't leave any notes behind." Asked by Summers whether Marilyn did leave a note, Gould says, "Yes, she did," adding that Lawford told her he had destroyed it.

This happened because Lawford went to Marilyn's house that night. According to Gould, "He went there and tidied up the place, and did what he could, before the police and the press arrived." Gould says Lawford destroyed the note "to protect loved ones involved"—the Kennedy brothers. "That's where Peter's role came in," Gould told Summers, "to cover up all the dirty work, and take care of everything."

Aftermath

More people came and went during the morning as the investigation went on, including police detectives and officials from the coroner's office. A coroner is a government official who determines the official cause of a death by conducting an autopsy—that is, by dissecting and analyzing a corpse.

The first one on the scene from the coroner's office, Guy Hockett, observed (as had Clemmons) that Monroe had been dead for several hours. For one thing, rigor mortis, the stiffening of muscles that occurs after death, was well advanced. Hockett later testified:

> It took about five minutes to straighten her out. . . . She was not lying quite straight, sort of in a semifetal [curled] position. . . . She didn't look good, not like Marilyn Monroe. She looked just like a poor little girl that had died, no makeup, fuzzy unmade hair, a tired body.

Hockett and his colleagues lifted Monroe's body from the bed and wheeled it outside on a gurney, a wheeled bed, covered by a blanket. They loaded their burden into a battered Ford panel truck and took it to a small mortuary, Westwood Village, next to the cemetery where Monroe's maternal grandmother was buried.

A few hours later Monroe's body was moved to crypt 33 at the county morgue in the Los Angeles Hall of Justice, and Marilyn Monroe become another statistic—Coroner's Case No. 81128.

Two photographers managed to sneak into the morgue that day. One, from the Los Angeles *Herald-Examiner*, secretly snapped a shot of the corpse with a hidden camera while a colleague covered the click of the shutter by flicking a cigarette lighter. The other, a freelancer who later sold his pictures to LIFE magazine, bribed an attendant with bottles of whiskey in order to get access to the body. These sad pictures were the last press photographs ever taken of Monroe's famous body.

The Police Investigation

Detective Sergeant Robert E. Byron was one of the many police officers who arrived on the scene Sunday morning. As senior officer, he assumed control of the case for the moment. It was to Byron that Murray changed the time of her discovery of the body to about 3:00 A.M. Byron was generally unimpressed with the statements he got from Murray, Greenson, and Engelberg. In his official

A coroner's truck containing Marilyn Monroe's body leaves her Hollywood home on the day of her death.

36

report, he noted, "It is officer's opinion that Mrs. Murray was vague and possibly evasive in answering questions pertaining to the activities of Miss Monroe during this time."

Greenson had told Clemmons that no one had found a suicide note, so plainclothes officer Don Marshall, one of the many police on the scene, was assigned to search thoroughly for a note. He spent several hours examining all the papers he could find in the house but found nothing that might have been a suicide note.

There have been reports over the years that a great number of papers were destroyed in the fireplace. There have also been stories that the locks on Monroe's metal filing cabinets were broken and that the drawers were open. The implication is that after her death someone destroyed sensitive documents that Monroe was keeping. However, Officer Marshall, who was on duty at the house all day, has consistently denied any knowledge of such action. As he put it, "Nobody was destroying anything."

As the morning progressed, the level of activity in the house increased. One visitor was Eunice Murray's son-in-law Norman Jeffries, who had done odd jobs for Monroe in the past. Murray summoned him to replace the pane of glass Ralph Greenson had shattered with the fireplace poker. Another morning visitor was Pat Newcomb, who stayed at Fifth Helena for about two hours before leaving to cope with the stream of calls that had begun to pour in from the press worldwide.

Coroners seal her house after Marilyn's body was removed from her home. Had Marilyn's body, and the evidence in her room, been tampered with? And if so, why?

By 8:30 A.M., the house was formally sealed. After that, only people authorized by the police were allowed in. Inez Melson, Monroe's business manager, was authorized to deal with the actress's personal belongings. She and her husband arrived the next day and found the bedside table still littered with pill bottles. Melson recalled in Anthony Summers's book *Goddess*:

> We found bottle after bottle after bottle. . . . There were sleeping pills, including Nembutal and Seconal. Whoever

had been there before us did not take them away. . . . We threw them all down the toilet, and I think I took the bottles away and put them in the garbage. . . . There've been many times since that I've wished I'd saved them.

The Autopsy

Meanwhile, deputy coroner Dr. Thomas Noguchi was performing an autopsy, a medical examination to determine the cause of death, on Monroe's remains. Noguchi eventually became the chief coroner for Los Angeles County and performed autopsies on many famous people, including Robert Kennedy, John Belushi, Natalie Wood, and Charles Manson victim Sharon Tate. In 1962, however, Noguchi was just beginning his career. He had been assigned to the case by the chief coroner of Los Angeles County, Dr. Theodore Curphey.

Observing Noguchi during the autopsy was John Miner, a deputy district attorney for Los Angeles County and chief of the district attorney's medical legal section. Miner, who also taught forensic psychiatry at the University of Southern California, was particularly respected for his skill in evaluating suicides and possible suicides. The findings and opinions of Noguchi and Miner would become crucial later in unraveling the mystery of Monroe's death.

Noguchi quickly determined that the actress's blood contained no alcohol at all. Monroe had never been a heavy drinker, indulging only in an occasional glass of champagne. Noguchi's analysis showed that she had not consumed any alcohol for at least several hours before her death.

Drugs, however, were another matter. Noguchi found 4.5 milligrams of barbiturate—specifically pentobarbital, the active ingredient in the sleeping pill Nembutal—and 8 milligrams percent of chloral hydrate in the blood. Chloral hydrate, commonly known as knockout drops, is also a sedative like Nembutal. Noguchi also found 13 milligrams percent of pentobarbital in the liver. Bottles containing both Nembutal and chloral hydrate were found at Monroe's house.

These percentages are extremely high—much higher than normal doses. Some pathologists have estimated that Monroe's Nembutal intake was roughly ten times the typical dose that might be

Dr. Thomas Noguchi was the deputy coroner of Los Angeles at the time of Marilyn Monroe's death. He performed the autopsy on Monroe's body, the first of many celebrity autopsies in his career.

prescribed by a doctor. The level of chloral hydrate in her system, meanwhile, was roughly twenty times the amount usually prescribed for sleep. Either drug, taken in such quantities, could have been fatal. Together, they were clearly enough to kill even someone whose system had become used to them through regular use.

Noguchi filed a preliminary autopsy report by 10:30 on the same Sunday morning as Monroe's death. On August 10, five days later, he submitted his final report. The cause of death was listed as "acute barbiturate poisoning due to ingestion of overdose." Under the heading Mode of Death, Noguchi circled the word *Suicide*, adding the word *probable* in his own handwriting. On August 17, chief coroner Theodore Curphey announced to the press that Monroe's death was a "probable suicide," and on August 27, Curphey made his final statement, repeating the verdict that Monroe's death was due to "acute barbiturate poisoning—ingestion of overdose."

Thus ended the official inquiry into the cause of Marilyn Monroe's death. As far as the police were concerned, the case was closed. However, this official investigation proved to be only the beginning. Even after more than thirty years and countless hours of research and speculation on the part of reporters and others who have become intrigued with Monroe's story, not all the questions raised have been answered. These researchers ask: Did she really commit suicide? Did she kill herself by accident? Did someone else accidentally kill her? Or, as some claim, was she murdered?

2 Did Marilyn Commit Suicide?

How can I capsulize Marilyn? The more you know about people the more complex they are to you. If she were simple, it would have been easy to help her.

former husband Arthur Miller

I did not think she committed suicide. [She was] not only making plans for the future but she felt that she had put everything bad behind her and could now go forward with her life.

assistant district attorney and forensic expert John Miner, 1992

From the very beginning, the official line from the Los Angeles police and from Monroe's studio publicity department was that Monroe's death had been a suicide. When the police arrived on the scene of Monroe's death, the first words out of Ralph Greenson's mouth were, "We lost her; she committed suicide." Police Chief William Parker, in his earliest press statement about the investigation, said, "Marilyn Monroe . . . took too many Nembutal capsules." The autopsy report made it official: death by barbiturate poisoning and probable suicide.

Several researchers, however, suspect that the official story is false for a number of reasons. These researchers believe that it is unlikely that Monroe killed herself. Furthermore, they suspect that the Los Angeles Police Department covered up the real cause of her death.

Was Suicide Likely?

Some investigators have pointed out reasons that it is unlikely Monroe would have been feeling desperate enough to take her own life.

Professionally, Monroe was at a peak. She was the biggest box office star in the world, and it did not seem likely that this status would change anytime soon. After completing *Something's Got to Give,* she was set to begin another film with Dean Martin immediately. Her production company, which she had kept alive after her partnership with Greene dissolved, was well on the road to making her long-awaited project, *The Jean Harlow Story.* Harlow was Marilyn's (and her mother's) lifelong idol, and this biographical film was a dream project for Monroe.

Although she suffered from depression throughout her life, at the time of her death Monroe seemed at a high point personally and professionally. If she was so content, why would she commit suicide?

She was riding especially high at the time of her death. Monroe was ecstatic that a series of seminude poolside photos taken on the set of *Something's Got to Give* were dominating magazine covers around the world. Her chief rival, Elizabeth Taylor, had recently gotten tremendous publicity for her role in *Cleopatra,* and Monroe was only too happy to take the limelight away from Taylor.

Her personal life was also better than it had been in years. She had begun to pull away from the dominant, controlling psychiatrist, who had played such a large role in her life, and to take control of her life in other ways as well, such as by firing Eunice Murray. She was living in a house that she loved and was only days away from marrying Joe DiMaggio for a second time. Monroe was finally close to establishing some much-needed stability in her life.

From this viewpoint Monroe's life seemed to be going well. On the other hand, it can be argued that the star was, in fact, a prime candidate for suicide. She had been insecure, depressed, and riddled with self-doubt for virtually her entire life. She had a maternal history of mental instability, including a great-grandfather who had committed suicide and a disturbed mother who would kill herself years after Monroe's death. There were rumors, never proven, that she had attempted suicide before, when married to Arthur Miller. She was addicted to pills that were seriously affecting her mood and

The Rich and Famous

This excerpt from Ralph Greenson's essay "Special Problems: Psychotherapy with the Rich and Famous," which he wrote after the death of Monroe, gives us a glimpse into what he thought of his famous client.

"Rich and famous people believe that prolonged psychotherapy is a rip-off. They want their therapist as a close friend, they even want their wife and their children to become part of the therapist's family. . . . These patients are seductive.

Rich and famous people need the therapist twenty-four hours a day and they are insatiable [unable to be satisfied]. They are also able to give you up completely in the sense they are doing to you what was done to them by their parents or their servants. You are their servant and can be dismissed without notice."

Marilyn leaves the hospital in 1961 after being hospitalized for depression. DiMaggio had arranged for her release after she was accidentally placed in a padded cell.

her judgment. She had recently undergone a traumatic experience in the New York hospital from which Joe DiMaggio rescued her, and that incident may have been a breakdown of sorts.

She had a history of failed marriages and she had been unable to have the child she desperately wanted. She had often been frustrated in her career—denied serious roles and tethered to a restrictive studio contract. There was intense public speculation and gossip that she was involved with powerful politicians and that her relationships with them were not going well.

The Suicide Prevention Team

Part of the police investigation in the first days following Monroe's death was the creation of a psychological profile of the actress.

Officials believed that this profile would help the coroner's office and the police determine if it was likely that she had indeed committed suicide. To this end, Chief Coroner Curphey asked the Los Angeles County Suicide Prevention Center for help. The team was composed of doctors, psychologists, and other experts in the area of suicide.

To the suicide prevention team, all the evidence pointed clearly toward a self-administered dose of drugs. In other words, it agreed with the coroner's office that Monroe committed suicide. The main evidence was the autopsy analysis that the cause of death was an overdose of Nembutal and chloral hydrate. This finding was consistent with evidence found at the scene of Monroe's death: a number of full or partly full bottles of drugs beside her bed, including an empty bottle that had contained twenty-five 100-milligram Nembutal capsules and a bottle with the remainder (ten capsules) of a prescription for fifty 500-milligram chloral hydrate capsules.

No Evidence of Injection

The team looked into but rejected the possibility that the drugs had been forcibly administered to Monroe. The autopsy found no evidence of an injection. Nor were there any signs of violence to Monroe's body or other indications that she had been held down so that someone could inject her. Noguchi did find two small bruises on her back, but he concluded that these had probably been caused when Monroe had bumped against the bed or nightstand in a drugged stupor.

The medical evidence given to the team clearly indicated a suicide. However, critics of the suicide verdict argue that the team's decision was affected by elements beyond the medical evidence. Some investigators believe that political pressure may have played a role.

First of all, critics point out, Curphey had believed all along that the case was suicide, and the team members would naturally be reluctant to disagree with the medically distinguished and politically connected chief coroner. These critics, including writer Donald Spoto, also point out that the team members never doubted the word of their respected colleague Ralph Greenson when he stated that Monroe's death was suicide. Spoto quotes Dr. Robert Litman, a member of the team, as saying, "It was obvious to us, after speaking with Dr. Greenson about Marilyn's psychiatric history, that the only conclusion we could reach was suicide, or at least a gamble with death." But this acceptance of Greenson's statements, critics point out, is at odds with the story told by Greenson and Murray and with some of the evidence at the death scene.

Finally, skeptics like writer Anthony Summers say that the team was feeling pressure to issue a quick decision. They claim to have evidence that authorities high up in government wanted to end the highly publicized affair and get it out of the public spotlight. They argue that the facts were covered up in order to close the case quickly. Exactly where this pressure might have come from has never been established. However, Dr. Litman stated (years later, to Donald Spoto) that the team was eager to close the case: "We wanted to get this over with, to come to a decision, close the case, issue a death certificate and move on. But of course, that turned out to be a misplaced hope. Nobody ever moved on."

Depressed?

Writer Fred Lawrence Guiles is one researcher who agrees with the conclusion that Monroe committed suicide. According to Guiles, near the end of her life the actress was having affairs with both John and Robert Kennedy. She committed suicide, he concluded,

Dr. Theodore Curphey, Los Angeles County coroner, declared Monroe's death a "probable suicide." Later investigators question whether Curphey came to this conclusion in an objective manner.

because she was severely depressed over her faltering relationships with the Kennedys, as well as her failed attempts to have a child.

Guiles suggested in his 1984 biography *Legend* that Monroe may have become pregnant by one of the Kennedys. He cites as evidence an interview with an unnamed employee of the Arthur Jacobs Agency, Monroe's publicity office. According to this source, during the weekend when she was supposed to be in Lake Tahoe with DiMaggio, Monroe was actually in a Mexican hospital undergoing an abortion. Guiles wrote, "It would be easy to assume that the aborted child was a Kennedy, but she was seeing other men as well that spring and summer." Guiles theorized that because Mar-

Many speculate that Marilyn may have had a relationship with one or both of the Kennedy brothers. Evidence links her to both President Kennedy (right) and his brother Robert.

"A Sense of Worthlessness"

Fred Guiles believes that Monroe deliberately killed herself over her broken affair with Robert Kennedy. In his book Legend: The Life and Death of Marilyn Monroe, *Guiles alleges that Monroe had also tried to kill herself while she was married to Arthur Miller.*

"Marilyn was a compulsive potential suicide. If Miller saved her three times after she actually had crossed the line of tolerance in her pill intake, consider what drove her to that point. Nothing visible, of course, only a sense of worthlessness that no amount of love and reassurance could overcome. And that last weekend she was in the grip of some final compulsion—a compulsion that had become determination. Was it the statement that Bobby Kennedy was making when he brought his family with him on his trip west to break off their affair, and Marilyn knew that Ethel and some of the children were just a short distance away?"

ilyn had yearned to have a child for many years, this abortion—which, he hinted, was made necessary by political pressure—may have added to her desperation.

Guiles concluded that Robert Kennedy called Monroe near the end of her life to say that he was coming to Los Angeles to make a final break with her. This phone call, Guiles suggested, is what caused her to take the fatal overdose. As he wrote:

> She had spent part of that Friday on the phone—as usual. In the early afternoon, she learned that Bobby Kennedy had left Washington for California. He had told her he was coming during their last phone conversation on Monday, July 30.

Guiles argued that Monroe then stockpiled a large quantity of pills by convincing both Greenson and Engelberg to give her prescriptions—clear evidence that she was deliberately planning her death. Guiles also quoted a story told by Eunice Murray about a disturbing scene that occurred beside the pool in Monroe's backyard on her last morning. According to Murray, Monroe was sitting beside the pool with Pat Newcomb when the actress suddenly turned to Murray and asked, "Do we have any oxygen?" Oxygen is

Did Marilyn commit suicide after Robert Kennedy (pictured) broke off his relationship with her?

often used to revive people who have tried to commit suicide by overdosing on pills. If this story is true, it strengthens the argument that Monroe was even then considering killing herself.

Did She Swallow the Pills?

If Monroe did commit suicide, the most likely method by far would have been with pills. Many investigators, however, do not believe this happened—or that she committed suicide by any other means. As writer Donald Spoto put it, "[S]uicide by deliberate Nembutal overdose would have been an action entirely inconsistent with everything in Marilyn Monroe's life at the time."

Spoto and others point out that it would have been virtually impossible for Monroe to give herself a fatal overdose by any other means than swallowing pills. No evidence of a syringe, for instance, was found at the death scene. On the other hand, they say, the likelihood of her swallowing the pills is extremely low. In his final press conference, Chief Coroner Curphey estimated she swallowed the pills in "one gulp within—let's say—a period of seconds." However, critics argue that this scenario is unlikely—and thus other possibilities open up.

Normally, these critics argue, a person who is committing suicide by taking an overdose of pills will wash them down with a drink. Surely, they say, the large number of pills Monroe would have had to take—estimates range from forty to eighty—would have required a large drink. But the police found no water glass (or evidence of any other liquid) on the table next to her bed. Furthermore, Monroe's bathroom, which opened off her bedroom, had no working plumbing that night because of the remodeling that was under way in her house. Eunice Murray did not mention Monroe's going to another room to get water at any point in her various interviews.

However, perhaps the most important evidence indicating that Monroe did not swallow the fatal dose is that the autopsy found no residue of capsules in her stomach. To many observers this fact is proof that the star did not swallow the overdose. Forty or fifty pills, they say, simply could not dissolve that quickly in the stomach; a trace of undigested drugs would have turned up in the autopsy. According to Dr. Arnold Abrams, medical director of pathology at St. John's Hospital in Santa Monica, California, and one of the pathologists consulted by biographer Donald Spoto, "The odds that she took pills and died from them are astronomically unlikely."

Why Were No Drugs in Her Stomach?

Another expert consulted by writer Anthony Summers was also bothered by the fact that Monroe's stomach was empty. Dr. Keith Simpson, emeritus professor in forensic medicine at London University, believed that the high levels of drugs in the blood and liver should have revealed a residue of capsules in the stomach. Simpson also noted the odd fact that no one examined Monroe's digestive tract, including the duodenum and the rest of the small bowel. An analysis of the digestive organs, Simpson said, would have solved the question. If the drugs had been swallowed, at least a small residue of the fatal drugs would have been found.

The reason that the digestive tract was not analyzed is unclear. Interviewed by Summers, Thomas Noguchi said he sent specimens of these organs to the toxicology laboratory but that they were never tested. At the time, Noguchi assumed that the chief toxicologist for Los Angeles County, Dr. Ralph Abenathy, had already found enough evidence in Monroe's blood and liver to create sufficient proof of the cause of death.

Furthermore, according to Noguchi, shortly after the case was formally closed Abenathy told him that the organ specimens had been destroyed. Noguchi told Summers:

> I should have insisted that all the organs be analyzed. But I didn't follow through as I should have. As a junior member of the staff, I didn't feel I could challenge the department heads on procedures.

To many observers, this revelation is just one of the many signs that important evidence in Monroe's autopsy and death report was destroyed or suppressed.

Her Final Despair

This excerpt from Anthony Summers's Goddess: The Secret Lives of Marilyn Monroe *cites testimony indicating that Monroe committed suicide over her broken relationship with Robert Kennedy.*

"Along with saying that Marilyn had recently had sexual relationships with 'extremely important men in government . . . at the highest level,' Dr. Greenson revealed [in testimony to the suicide prevention team] that on [her final] Saturday afternoon she expressed considerable dissatisfaction with the fact that here she was, the most beautiful woman in the world, and she did not have a date for Saturday night.

According to one suicide team doctor, Norman Tabachnick, Greenson said Marilyn had been expecting to see one of the 'very important people' that night. She had called Greenson when she learned the meeting was off. Marilyn died, Greenson said, feeling 'rejected by some of the people she had been close to.'

Sometime before she called Greenson that day . . . Marilyn had learned she would not be seeing Robert Kennedy in the evening. That, on the evidence, triggered her final despair."

Glamorous Marilyn Monroe seemed to have everything: fame, fortune, and massive public appeal. However, her many doomed relationships with men may have led her to take her own life.

The Last Meal

Other experts argue that a lack of drugs in Monroe's stomach does not necessarily indicate foul play. In 1982 Dr. Boyd Stephens, chief medical examiner for the city of San Francisco, offered his opinions during an official review of the case for the Los Angeles district attorney's office. Stephens pointed out that although remnants of capsules are often found in the stomachs of suicide victims, this is not always the case. The results depend on several factors. These include the time of the victim's last meal; how much liquid was consumed in the hours before death; the victim's individual metabolism (rate of absorbing drugs or food); whether the victim was a regular drug user with a high tolerance; and whether the drug was taken at one time or over a period of hours.

One of the most crucial of these factors is the time of the last meal. In Monroe's case, there is conflicting evidence concerning the last meal. Eunice Murray testified that Monroe did not eat at all on her last day alive. However, Pat Newcomb recalled her eating a hamburger at lunch. Apparently, Monroe had no dinner; no one mentions her eating after lunch. By evening, in any case, her stomach would have been virtually empty, and her system would probably have quickly absorbed the barbiturates. This theory is consistent with the autopsy report that found no trace of capsules in her stomach.

Another crucial factor was the rate at which her body could absorb drugs. This rate is, in large part, a factor of how high a dosage she was accustomed to taking and thus how much her system could absorb in a given amount of time. Monroe had taken sleeping pills for years. Anthony Summers quotes several of Monroe's friends recalling that she regularly took high dosages without serious effect. If this observation is true, Marilyn probably had developed a high tolerance for sleeping pills and would quickly absorb them. This theory is also consistent with the autopsy report.

Cover-Up?

In the days following Monroe's death, the official investigation moved quickly. The day after Curphey asked the suicide prevention team for help, the center's founder, Dr. Norman Farberow, told reporters, "We are interviewing anybody and everybody. We will go as far back as is necessary." It seemed likely that the inquiry would take its time and explore every possibility. Three days later, implying the possibility of foul play, the New York *Herald Tribune* headline screamed WHAT KILLED MARILYN? PROBE WIDENS.

Then, quite suddenly, the investigation slowed. Within a week of Monroe's death, newspapers were reporting hints of pressure to shut down the investigation. Shortly afterwards, Coroner Curphey announced his official verdict of "probable suicide." Later investigators are suspicious of this sudden closure. They believe it indicates a cover-up.

The man ultimately responsible for the inquiry into Monroe's death was Police Chief William Parker. He ordered his detectives to pay special attention to the case, because of Monroe's fame and because of the gossip that she was close to the Kennedys.

Parker was a nationally respected officer with a reputation for integrity. However, many investigators have claimed that the Los Angeles police—and Parker in particular—were involved in a massive cover-up of the facts surrounding Monroe's death. There have been allegations that Parker suppressed a secret report on Monroe and the Kennedys, but no proof has ever surfaced to support the claim. Allegedly, Parker buried the case in order to gain favor with the Kennedy family, whom he knew.

Some have charged that Police Chief William Parker was part of a massive cover-up as to the true cause of Marilyn's death.

Autopsy surgeon Thomas Noguchi is one authority who has remained troubled by the Monroe investigation. Even many years after the fact, he suspected that some sort of cover-up had taken place. Quoted in Anthony Summers's book, Noguchi said:

> [I] had the strong feeling that the case was being delayed, and that the scene of death had been disturbed. . . . It seemed to me, from all I observed, that it's very likely the Police Department did close things down [prematurely]. I've encountered this often in my experience, in deaths involving important people.

In 1982 the Los Angeles Board of Supervisors asked the district attorney's office to review the case. The purpose was to determine if there was enough evidence of a cover-up to warrant reopening

Years after Marilyn's death, former coroner's aide Lionel Grandison cast suspicion on the investigation in 1982 by saying that he was coerced to sign Marilyn's death certificate when he knew that it was "murder" and not suicide.

the investigation. The board was responding to the allegations of a former coroner's aide named Lionel Grandison.

Grandison alleged evidence had been suppressed from the autopsy. Specifically, he claimed that Monroe's body had massive bruises that were not noted on the report. Assistant District Attorney Ronald Carroll, who was in charge of the 1982 review, did not find Grandison a believable witness. In fact, Grandison had been fired from the coroner's office amid allegations that he had stolen property from corpses awaiting autopsies. The district attorney's office concluded that "based on the information available, no further criminal investigation appears required into Miss Monroe's death."

If Marilyn Monroe did commit suicide, many puzzling questions remain. Perhaps, some observers say, she died by accident; perhaps she simply took an overdose of sleeping pills by mistake. Meanwhile, some researchers have claimed that her death was indeed caused by an accidental overdose—but that the accidental overdose was given to her by someone else. The persistent rumors of a police cover-up increase the likelihood that Monroe's death was something other than a desperate suicide.

3 Did She Die Accidentally?

Marilyn wasn't killed by Hollywood. It was the goddamn doctors who killed her. If she was a pill addict, they made her so.

director John Huston

She was a poor creature I tried to help, and I ended up hurting her.

Dr. Ralph Greenson

The official police report, which concluded that Monroe committed suicide, did not rule on whether the death was accidental or whether she deliberately killed herself. However, in the weeks following Monroe's death, the story given to the press by her studio and her publicity agency was clear and unambiguous: Marilyn Monroe had taken her own life by mistake.

According to this official version, which is the version a stunned public heard and accepted, Monroe had taken a sedative early in the evening and had fallen asleep. She then woke up in the middle of the night. Groggy and disoriented, she took another dose—not realizing that she was adding to her earlier medication and creating an overdose. In the words of Monroe's personal publicist, Pat Newcomb, "There was a terrible accident."

A Slow Death

Dr. Keith Simpson, the forensic pathologist consulted by Anthony Summers, agrees with the verdict of accidental overdose. He cited the absence of drug residue in her stomach combined with the high level of drugs found in her liver. These factors together indicate that the fatal dose began several hours before her death, since they apparently had time to move from the stomach to the liver. Simpson also cited Ralph Greenson's testimony that Monroe had seemed "somewhat drugged" on the afternoon before her death as

Investigators speculated that Monroe had accidentally overdosed by ingesting barbiturates throughout her last day. This would rule her death an accident.

evidence that the process of increasing the drug dosage occurred over several hours.

Simpson's conclusion was that Monroe had ingested the barbiturates gradually throughout the course of her last day. These drugs could have stayed in her bloodstream for up to twelve hours. He also suggested that Monroe took a final dose, not realizing that the combined effect would be lethal, later in the evening. He pointed out that, considering the amount of barbiturates already in her system, the last dose of fifteen pills or so would have proved fatal. As he put it, "She may have [not realized] the cumulative effect of the pills taken earlier. In that case, her death may have been not suicide, but a tragic mistake."

Dr. Noguchi, interviewed for the Summers book, agreed that Monroe had taken at least some of the drugs he found during the autopsy several hours before dying. He cited as evidence the high level of drugs in her liver and the relatively low level in her blood. This evidence indicates that much of the Nembutal reached the liver during Monroe's last day and that the process of digesting it had already begun.

The conclusions of both Simpson and Noguchi are in direct contradiction to Coroner Curphey's public announcement at the time of the official inquiry. Curphey stated that Monroe had swallowed all her pills at once, probably within the space of a few seconds. If that had happened, however, there would have been little or no trace of drugs in her liver, since they would not have had time to be absorbed, and there would have been at least some residue in her stomach.

The suicide prevention team, in preparing its report at the time of Monroe's death, had also considered the possibility that she took an overdose by accident. However, it rejected this conclusion as unlikely. The team assumed that an accident would have occurred for one of two reasons: either because Monroe was psychotic (in which case she would not have realized what she was doing) or because she was a very heavy drug addict (in which case she could have overdosed while thinking she was taking a safe amount). The team rejected both possibilities. Spoto quotes Dr. Norman Farberow, a member of the team: "Her intake [of drugs] could be considered light to medium. And she was certainly not mentally unbalanced so far as I could determine."

Some investigators disagree with the explanation that Monroe took too much medication by accident on the grounds that Monroe had been using sleeping pills for many years. She was an expert in combining them and in knowing what their cumulative effect would be. It is unlikely, they say, that even in a groggy and disoriented state she could have made such a serious mistake.

Injection?

Some researchers, including Robert Slatzer, have suggested that the drugs found in Monroe's body were administered by injection.

They point to the autopsy report, which noted a lack of drugs in Monroe's kidneys. This pattern indicates that the stomach was completely bypassed when the drug took effect, which is what would happen in the case of an injection.

However, other autopsy evidence makes it seem unlikely that an injection was the cause of death. In addition to the fact that no syringe or needle was found on the scene, the medical evidence also points away from injection. For one thing, Noguchi carefully ex-

Sleeping, Waking Up

In this excerpt from Marilyn Monroe: The Biography, *Donald Spoto reflects on the ease of obtaining and using drugs in Monroe's world of filmmaking.*

"Chemical dependence was poorly understood as late as the 1960s; it was also something Marilyn's colleagues, employers and friends did little to correct. Barbiturates to sleep, amphetamines to stay awake, narcotics to relax—in Hollywood, these were as plentiful as agents, and could easily be obtained through the studio front office. Bookshelves are heavy with horror tales of film stars' lives imperiled or destroyed by careless physicians working for uncaring studio executives who ordered whatever was necessary to get a performer through a production. Errol Flynn, Judy Garland, Tyrone Power, Montgomery Clift, Richard Burton, Elizabeth Taylor— the names are legion and stretch from the days of silent film to the time of music video. . . .

Yet of all movie stars, Marilyn Monroe's reputation has suffered the most—perhaps because of her fundamental benevolence, her youth, her simplicity, her patent longing to belong. Such a woman, to whom the fantasies and hopes of an entire culture were attached, was disallowed weakness. She had to be as perfect as her onscreen beauty, her strength as unmarred as her face, the blond halo a sign of inner perfection: the culture was asking more of Marilyn Monroe than perhaps of anyone in its popular history. And because she was a woman, she seemed to fail twice as badly, to disappoint infinitely more than the tipsy chaps at the bar or the playboys sneaking in and out of Beverly Hills bedrooms."

amined every inch of Monroe's body with a magnifying glass and found no evidence of injection, such as a puncture wound.

Also, a massive injection of drugs leaves a bruise. A bruise gradually disappears from the skin—unless the person dies, in which case it remains visible. Since death would have occurred immediately with a large dose of drugs, any injection-induced bruise on Monroe's skin would have been clearly visible during the autopsy. The only bruises found on Monroe's body, however, were two light bruises on her lower back. They indicated to Noguchi that she had perhaps stumbled slightly against the bed or nightstand at some point during the evening.

Finally, the relative amounts of drugs found in her bloodstream and liver point away from the possibility of death by injection. If she had died that way, the drugs would have been absorbed very quickly into the system. There would have been no time for them to reach the liver, and so there would have been a higher concentration in the blood and less in the liver than was found during the autopsy.

All of this information combines with the police evidence—that there were no syringes or needles—to make death by injection an unlikely scenario. In its 1982 review of the case, the Los Angeles district attorney's office noted, "This [the evidence] leads to a reasonable conclusion that Miss Monroe had not suffered a 'hot shot' or needle injection of a lethal dose."

Enema?

The only other way Monroe's fatal dose could have been administered, besides swallowing pills or injection, could have been by means of a rectal enema.

An enema is a procedure in which a liquid is introduced into the lower digestive tract by inserting a tube in the rectum. This method allows the medicine to be distributed quickly into the digestive system. Enemas have been a common procedure for many years for general hygienic purposes, for relief from health problems such as constipation, or for a quick, short-term weight loss. Normally enemas are not used to deliver strong medication such as barbiturates because the impact of medication is much stronger when delivered this way and the danger of an accidental overdose is greater.

Enemas were a popular health fad among members of the movie colony in the 1950s and 1960s. For years, Monroe had relied on them regularly. She suffered from chronic constipation, and she also frequently used enemas to lose weight quickly so that she could fit into an especially tight gown. As writer Donald Spoto put it, for Monroe taking an enema for constipation or weight loss was "as casual a habit as a haircut or shampoo and far more dangerous."

During the autopsy, Noguchi discovered an unusual condition, one that observer John Miner stated was unique among the thousands of autopsies he has participated in. This strange condition has given weight to the possibility that Monroe's fatal dose was delivered by this third method.

The unusual condition was a gross discoloration of a portion of the digestive system called the sigmoid colon. According to Noguchi's report, Monroe's sigmoid colon bore "marked congestion and purplish discoloration," which indicated that she had recently been given an enema and that something in the enema had caused the severe congestion. In Donald Spoto's book, John Miner stated that this condition was abnormal and added, "Noguchi and I were convinced that an enema was absolutely the route of administering the fatal drug dose."

It is a remote possibility that Monroe might have somehow given herself an enema. According to some experts, however, the odds against this happening are huge. It would be far too much trouble to self-administer, especially for someone who was distraught and confused; it is much easier and more common for a suicide to simply swallow pills.

A related possibility is that the drugs were administered by suppository. This type of medication is inserted a short way into the rectum, where it dissolves and is absorbed. Some investigators have suggested that Monroe took Nembutal suppositories. However, others point out that a suppository would reach only a short way into the anus and would not have caused any discoloration of the sigmoid colon.

Did Someone Else Accidentally Kill Her?

The only possible conclusion, according to Donald Spoto, is that someone else administered the enema. However, as Spoto points out, even if it could be established that Monroe received a fatal enema, two questions remain: What was the drug, and who gave the enema?

Two drugs, Nembutal and chloral hydrate, were found in Monroe's system. However, the question of exactly which drug killed her remains unclear. Although no one can say for certain, it appears that the lethal drug was the chloral hydrate. Ralph Greenson testified that he had stopped prescribing Nembutal for Monroe some time before her death. He was trying to reduce her dependence on the drug in favor of chloral hydrate, which he felt was safer. He had asked Hyman Engelberg, Monroe's regular physician, not to prescribe Nembutal for her without his permission.

However, Engelberg testified that on the day before her death he gave Monroe a prescription for Nembutal without Greenson's knowledge. He said that Monroe had convinced him it would be all right. Two weeks after Monroe's death, Greenson corroborated this story in a letter to Marianne Kris, Monroe's New York psychiatrist:

> On Friday night she had told the internist [Engelberg] that I had said it was all right for her to take some Nembutal, and he had given it to her without checking with me, because he had been upset for his own personal reasons. He had just left his wife.

During their final sessions on Saturday, Greenson had noticed that Monroe was "somewhat drugged." This may have been the Nembutal, which she had taken without Greenson's knowledge.

However, when Greenson was preparing to leave Monroe's house, she was still awake, angry, and difficult to manage. Donald Spoto has suggested that Greenson gave her a further sedative—chloral hydrate, his drug of choice for her. This theory fits with the medical evidence. The relative levels of chloral hydrate and Nembutal found in Monroe's blood and liver indicate that the chloral hydrate was taken some time after the Nembutal.

According to Spoto, when Greenson gave her the chloral hydrate he did not know that she had already taken a high dose of Nembutal, and he carelessly overlooked a crucial factor: that the two drugs could interact adversely. Chloral hydrate prevents the body from metabolizing (processing) Nembutal correctly; taken together in the wrong dosages, the combination is deadly. Green-

Dr. Greenson is the one man most implicated in Marilyn's death. Some say he was the one who gave Marilyn a fatal overdose, then lied to cover it up.

65

son apparently realized too late what he had done; shortly after Monroe's death, John Miner reported, the psychiatrist sadly told him, "If only I'd known about that other prescription."

Did the Housekeeper Do It?

According to Spoto's theory, the fatal dose was administered not by Greenson, but by Eunice Murray acting on his orders. Spoto suggested that, since Monroe was resisting further oral medication, Greenson decided to give the added medication via enema. Monroe would not necessarily have been alarmed at the suggestion, and chances are good that she did not realize that a chloral hydrate enema could be dangerous, even fatal, when added to Nembutal.

Spoto gave several reasons why the culprit was likely to be Murray. The housekeeper was extremely dependent on both Monroe, her famous boss, and Greenson, who for fifteen years had befriended her and found her employment. According to a number of Murray's relatives, as well as Monroe's friends, Murray always followed Greenson's orders closely.

Greenson, meanwhile, did not usually administer medicine himself to his patients; he let others, such as Dr. Engelberg, perform the task. In the absence of Engelberg, Greenson might well have asked Murray to give an enema. According to Spoto, because Murray had no special training in nursing, it would have been easy for her to accidentally give the actress an overdose. Spoto hints that Murray may have subconsciously given Monroe an overdose on purpose, since she was angry and upset over having recently been fired.

Spoto also pointed to Murray's strange behavior during the first hours after the police arrived; she was doing the laundry. Even when Monroe was in a coma, an enema would have been expelled at some point; there would be no reason for Murray to wash the sheets, Spoto argued, unless they had been soiled. It is possible that she was simply keeping busy with mindless tasks during a traumatic period, but she could also have been covering up guilty actions.

Details, Details

This scenario—a terrible accident resulting from the careless administration of what was meant to be a calming sedative—would explain the long delay between the time Murray discovered the body and the time Greenson called the police. Perhaps Monroe

Marilyn's housekeeper, Eunice Murray, found Marilyn dead. Her inconsistent testimony to police investigators cast aspersions on her credibility.

was still alive, and Greenson and Engelberg tried to revive her by pumping her stomach. As novelist Norman Mailer pointed out in his book-length essay on Monroe, an attempt to revive her would account for Monroe's empty stomach and intestines.

On the other hand, as Spoto suggested, perhaps the guilty parties spent the missing hours covering their trail. Even if the doctor and the housekeeper had not spent the time pumping her stomach, there would be dozens of details to arrange in order to make the death look like suicide. They would have needed to take care of the bedsheets and tidy up the room; they would have needed to deliberately break the bedroom window, remove the blackout fab-

Highly Improbable

In this excerpt from Anthony Summers's Goddess: The Secret Lives of Marilyn Monroe, *the writer cites an interview between Deputy District Attorney John Miner and Dr. Ralph Greenson involving the possibility that Monroe committed suicide, accidental or not.*

"The Deputy District Attorney came away from Dr. Greenson's office in professional confusion. What he learned, he says, persuaded him it was 'highly improbable' Marilyn deliberately killed herself. 'Among other things,' says Miner, 'it was clear that she had plans and expectations for her immediate future.' He will neither confirm nor deny that these plans involved one of the Kennedys. Asked if Dr. Greenson thought Marilyn was murdered, Miner says, 'That is something on which I cannot respond.' In August 1962, as a Deputy District Attorney, Miner had to report on the Greenson interview. What he did was to write a memorandum, which he recalls roughly as follows:

> As requested by you I have been to see Dr. Greenson to discuss the death of his late patient Marilyn Monroe. We discussed this matter for a period of hours, and as a result of what Dr. Greenson told me, and from what I heard on tape recordings [of sessions between Monroe and Greenson], I believe I can say definitely that it was not suicide."

ric from the window (which was found by the police neatly folded nearby), and carefully rehearse their story.

If they indeed were responsible for an accidental death, Greenson and Murray had little choice but to cover up their actions. To admit responsibility would have been disastrous. For one thing, to admit that he had allowed the untrained and unqualified Murray to give Monroe a lethal enema would have ruined Greenson's career. It is also unlikely that Murray, as dependent as she was on Greenson and on her connection with Monroe, could have brought herself to admit any guilt.

Several researchers cite as evidence of the truth of this scenario discrepancies between the first story that Murray, Greenson, and

Engelberg gave to police and the various versions they gave later. These discrepancies, according to researcher Robert Slatzer, indicate that the doctors and the housekeeper were hiding the true cause of death from the very beginning.

The most glaring example of conflicting information concerns the time at which Murray noticed something was wrong. When first questioned, she told Sergeant Clemmons that it was midnight. Later that morning when interviewed by Detective Sergeant Byron, and in all other interviews, she changed the critical time to 3:00 A.M.

Murray told Clemmons that she had been alerted by a light under Monroe's door and tried to arouse Monroe by knocking once. However, she told Byron that she tried knocking twice—the first time before 3:30 A.M. on her way to the bathroom and again shortly after 3:30, when she noticed the light was still on and the door locked. In a follow-up report to police, she gave still another version: that she had knocked twice, once before phoning Greenson and once after.

Murray also told Clemmons that she had phoned Greenson only one time. However, she told Byron that she had called Greenson twice, once after getting no response to her knock and again after seeing Monroe through the window. In a later interview, she repeated the two-phone-call version of her story.

Meanwhile, Greenson's stories also have conflicting details. He told Clemmons that he was the first to see Monroe's body. He told both Byron and the follow-up interviewer, however, that Murray had been the first. Concerning another detail, Greenson told both Clemmons and Byron that he had called Engelberg after breaking the window and finding Monroe. In the third interview, however, he stated that he told Murray to call Engelberg before he (Greenson) left his own home.

Furthermore, according to the initial interviews with Clemmons, none of the three witnesses mentioned a telephone in Monroe's hand. However, Greenson later told Byron that he removed the telephone receiver from Monroe's hand when he found her. He repeated that statement in a follow-up interview.

No Light?

The discrepancies in Murray's story keep piling up. According to Donald Spoto, a light could not possibly have shone under Monroe's door, as the housekeeper stated. Brand new, deep-pile, white carpeting had recently been installed in her bedroom. It was so thick that it prevented the door from closing completely, until a slightly pushed-down arc could be worn into the carpet. Therefore, no light could have been seen beneath the door. Confronted with this fact later, Murray quickly changed her story to say that she became alarmed when she noticed the telephone cord leading under the door. Murray claimed that Monroe never slept with the phone in her room, because she was afraid of being disturbed.

Another contradiction was Murray's statement that the bedroom door was locked. In fact, Monroe's door had never had an operating lock, a point which Murray admitted years later. Monroe never locked her bedroom door; this had been a lifelong habit.

Moreover, the story that Murray parted the draperies of Monroe's bedroom window with a fireplace poker is, according to Spoto, impossible. The window coverings were not draperies but a single piece of heavy blackout fabric, nailed beyond both sides of the window by Ralph Roberts soon after Marilyn moved in. There was no part in the middle for Eunice to push aside even if the windows had been open.

Ralph Greenson never spoke in public about the death of Monroe except to repeat the story he had told the police, and he never wrote about it. Eunice Murray, meanwhile, continued to give occasional interviews. She never admitted any role in Monroe's death, however, and never pointed an accusing finger at Greenson. The housekeeper's book about her experiences, which she wrote many years later, casts her in a clear and blameless light.

Considering the possibility that Monroe was killed by someone else—that she did not commit suicide—opens up new areas of speculation. Perhaps it was a terrible accident caused by a doctor's carelessness, as Donald Spoto suggested. Perhaps, however, as several other researchers contend, something much more sinister happened on that summer night on Fifth Helena Drive. Perhaps, they say, someone murdered Marilyn Monroe.

Was She Murdered?

There was a Coroner's investigation, and it was flawed. There was a police investigation, and there was a cover-up.

writer Anthony Summers

The facts, as we have found them, do not support a finding of foul play.

Los Angeles District Attorney
John Van de Kamp following a
1982 inquiry into Monroe's death

Since very shortly after the death of Marilyn Monroe, there have been persistent rumors that it was not a suicide or a tragic accident. These rumors hint at something far more sinister: murder. Although proof has never been found, new allegations about Monroe's death appear regularly in the press.

The method of the murder and the motive, that is, the reason behind it, differ greatly, depending on who is creating the theory. Generally, however, the charges that Monroe was murdered involve a complicated plot with a colorful cast of entertainment celebrities, organized crime bosses, and high government officials. According to this theory, Monroe had become what novelist Dominick Dunne once called "an inconvenient woman"—a troublemaker who had to be silenced by shadowy, powerful figures.

The Link with John Kennedy

Monroe became intensely interested in Democratic politics toward the end of her life. She was also active in such liberal issues as civil rights. She worked hard to educate herself on current affairs, and she enjoyed talking with friends and acquaintances about the important topics of the day.

She had always enjoyed the company of powerful men and was proud of her friendships with President John F. Kennedy and Attorney General Robert F. Kennedy. The charismatic John Kennedy, who had been a regular visitor to Hollywood's movie colony since his days as a U.S. senator, always enjoyed the company of beautiful women. There are many stories of an alleged affair between Monroe and JFK, and lack of proof that the affair ever took place has never silenced the rumors.

One book on Monroe, *Marilyn: The Last Take* by entertainment writers Peter Harry Brown and Patte B. Barham, quoted Hazel Washington, Monroe's studio maid, as saying, "She slept with him [JFK] off and on—whenever there was a scrap of time." Brown and Barham also alluded to secret meetings between the famous couple aboard *Air Force One* (the official presidential jet), at the Santa Monica home of Kennedy's brother-in-law Peter Lawford, and at a bachelor apartment that the married Kennedy maintained in New York. Writer Anthony Summers, meanwhile, also accepted the Monroe-Kennedy affair as truth. In his book *Goddess*, Summers quoted Peter Lawford's third wife as stating that Kennedy's affair with Monroe began before he became president and continued during his tenure in the White House.

Biographer Donald Spoto, however, has pointed out that there is no hard evidence to prove the affair ever took place. If it did occur, Spoto argues, it was a very brief affair. All that can be proven beyond a doubt is that John Kennedy and Marilyn Monroe met four times between October 1961 and August 1962. On only one of those occasions, according to Spoto, can it be clearly demonstrated that they were alone. On this occasion, Monroe phoned her masseur friend Ralph Roberts. She told him she was calling from a bedroom at the home of Bing Crosby in Palm Springs, where Kennedy was a houseguest. She told Roberts she was with a friend who suffered from chronic back pain and wanted some advice. Monroe handed the phone over to the friend, who turned out to be the president of the United States.

The Link with Robert Kennedy

John Kennedy's role as a playboy, though rumored for many years while he was living, has received public attention only recently. In contrast, the reputation of his younger brother Robert has always been that of a moral, straight-arrow, family man who never en-

John F. Kennedy and Peter Lawford at the Kennedy house in Palm Beach, Florida, in 1955. Some investigators still argue that it was JFK that had Marilyn murdered.

gaged in outside affairs. Yet among Monroe-conspiracy buffs, the rumors that the actress was involved with Robert Kennedy are, if anything, even more persistent than the rumors of her affair with the president. Despite the lack of proof, dozens of stories link Monroe to RFK. They began in the period following Monroe's death in 1962 and preceding RFK's assassination in 1968.

The first public accusation came in 1964 when Frank Capell, a right-wing political activist, published a book that claimed both Robert Kennedy and Marilyn Monroe were part of a communist

The New Item

In 1985 a BBC film team researching a show on Monroe and the Kennedys found what it claimed was a handwritten note from Jean Kennedy Smith, the sister of Robert and John Kennedy, to Marilyn Monroe. The alleged note, which bore the address of the Kennedy compound in Palm Beach, Florida, read:

"Dear Marilyn:

Mother asked me to write and thank you for your sweet note to Daddy—he really enjoyed it and you were very cute to send it. Understand that you and Bobby are the new item! We all think you should come with him when he comes back.

Love,
Jean Smith"

In his book Goddess: The Secret Lives of Marilyn Monroe, *Anthony Summers commented:*

"Assuming the note is genuine, what does it mean? It is undated, but there may be a clue in the reference to Marilyn's 'sweet note to Daddy.' 'Daddy,' seventy-three-year-old Joseph Kennedy, had suffered a serious stroke on December 19, 1961, at Palm Beach. . . .

Timing aside, what does one make of the provocative sentence, "Understand that you and Bobby are the new item!" Was this a wry jest, uttered in light of some public gossip linking Marilyn and Robert Kennedy? Hardly. There was no such gossip at this stage. Did this then mean exactly what it said, in the vernacular [slang] of the period? Was Jean Kennedy cheerfully acknowledging an affair, a dalliance of some sort, between Marilyn and her brother?"

conspiracy. At the time, America was deep in the cold war with the Soviet Union, and right-wing groups feared a secret communist takeover of the United States.

In his book, Capell claimed that Monroe was furious because RFK was trying to end their affair, and she was threatening to expose him as a communist sympathizer. Kennedy then ordered Monroe's death by "deploying his personal Gestapo." Capell also suggested that Ralph Greenson, Hyman Engelberg, and Eunice Murray were also fellow travelers, the term right-wing groups used to describe communist sympathizers.

Capell furthered his cause when he hooked up with a fellow communist-hater, Jack Clemmons, the same man, since retired, who was the first policeman to arrive at the scene of Monroe's death. Capell and Clemmons fed allegations about RFK and Monroe to influential New York gossip columnist Walter Winchell. Winchell published the rumors as if they were fact, though he identified RFK only as a "powerful man" and dropped hints as to his true identity.

Nothing in print identified Kennedy by name until 1973, after RFK's assassination. When novelist Norman Mailer published his book-length essay on Monroe to accompany a series of photos, he voiced some of the stories that had been circulating for the previous decade. These included rumors that neighbors of the Lawfords in Santa Monica often saw Monroe and RFK on the beach together, that RFK landed secretly by helicopter at Lawford's house on the day of Monroe's death, and that a group of women gathered at Monroe's neighbor's house for a bridge game saw Robert Kennedy entering Monroe's house on the day she died.

Mailer's book opened the floodgates for scores of other writers who linked Monroe with the Kennedys. In the opinion of Donald Spoto, such rumors have tarnished the reputations of both people. When they were mere speculation, he wrote, the stories could be dismissed as fantasy; the danger arose when a distinguished writer like Mailer gave them credence, at which point the public began accepting the rumors as truth. As Spoto put it, "The attorney general was unjustly transformed in the public's mind from a compassionate champion of civil rights to a darkly amoral character willing to kill for his reputation."

Was RFK There?

One rumor about Robert Kennedy was that he visited Monroe on the last day of her life. According to official FBI records, Kennedy was in northern California that weekend with his family. They arrived on Friday and stayed at the ranch of a friend, attorney John Bates. On the following Monday, RFK addressed a convention of lawyers in San Francisco. According to RFK's host, the entire Kennedy family was at the Bates's house all weekend, and it would have been impossible for RFK to make a seven-hundred-mile round trip to Los Angeles in secret. Quoted in the Spoto book, Bates testified:

> The attorney general and his family were with us every minute from Friday after noon to Monday, and there is simply no physical way that he could have gone to Southern California and returned.

The evidence seems to support this statement. For one thing, the nearest airstrip to Bates's ranch at Mount Madonna was an hour away. Adding this time to the time it would take to fly to Los Angeles and back would have created a large gap in Kennedy's schedule. A helicopter flight in and out of the mountainous region around the Bates ranch would have been dangerous and would certainly have been noticed. The only practical way to travel in secret from the Bates ranch to Los Angeles would have been by car—at least a five-hour trip each way—and Kennedy was never absent for that long.

Witnesses Place Kennedy in L.A.

And yet many people report seeing Kennedy in Los Angeles that weekend. According to one witness, RFK was dining at the fashionable La Scala restaurant with Monroe that Saturday night. Another report has him at the Beverly Hilton Hotel on the same night. Still another has him arriving by helicopter at Lawford's beachfront house. And one, reported by writers Peter Harry Brown and Patte B. Barham, says that Kennedy was at Monroe's house that afternoon, where they held hands and walked around the pool. Brown and Barham alleged that Monroe made secret recordings of the conversation between herself and Kennedy, which eventually made their way to high government officials:

> Sound recordings of that visit probably exist somewhere in the vaults of the Secret Service, the CIA or the FBI. J. Edgar Hoover was said to have made a copy for his own secret files, and apparently listened to it regularly.

Brown concluded that Robert Kennedy, shaken by Monroe's threat to publicize their affair, secretly flew to Los Angeles on the weekend of her death. Brown claimed that Kennedy and an unnamed doctor gave Monroe a strong sedative early in the evening. Later that evening, someone administered a potent shot of Nembu-

Robert Slatzer, author of The Life and Curious Death of Marilyn Monroe. *Slatzer claimed to have been secretly married to Marilyn.*

tal. Monroe was dead by 10:00 P.M., according to this scenario, and Peter Lawford spearheaded the massive cover-up that followed.

On the other hand, Brown also took seriously the theory that the CIA arranged Monroe's murder. He wrote, "Because of Monroe's loose words on the plot to kill Fidel Castro, the CIA had a strong stake in her demise." He also pointed to a series of articles published on the twenty-fifth anniversary of Monroe's death by the Soviet newspaper agency TASS. According to these articles, newly available information from the KGB, the Soviet secret service, revealed that the CIA killed Monroe because she planned to expose an American plot to murder Cuban dictator Fidel Castro. As Brown wrote, "The theory is not farfetched."

One of the most startling allegations about RFK and Monroe came from Robert Slatzer in his 1974 book *The Life and Curious Death of Marilyn Monroe.* Slatzer has made a career out of writing books and appearing on talk shows, all the while claiming that he was one of Monroe's closest friends and was even secretly married to her for a brief period. Although there is no proof that he met Monroe more than once, when he was a visitor on the set of the film *Niagara,* a number of researchers take his claims seriously.

Slatzer went further than simply accusing RFK of arranging Monroe's murder. He asserted that Robert Kennedy played a more direct role in her death. Slatzer claimed that he had knowledge of a secret statement that Kennedy gave to the Los Angeles Police Department. According to this, a hysterical phone call from Monroe summoned RFK and an unidentified doctor to Monroe's house on the afternoon before her death. The confrontation between Monroe and RFK soon became violent. At one point, he knocked down the raging Monroe and then held her still as the unidentified doctor injected a fatal tranquilizer under her armpit.

The Red Diary and the Tapes

Many other speculators have proposed their own variations of the Monroe-RFK link. One of them, Lionel Grandison, a former coroner's aide, claimed in 1982 that the autopsy report was falsified and that records indicating extensive bruising have been suppressed. Although the district attorney's investigation that followed Grandison's accusations disqualified him as a credible witness, Grandison has continued to make public allegations about Monroe. He has since claimed knowledge of a phony suicide note, which was meant to reinforce the suicide theory but which disappeared from a locker in the coroner's office shortly after the actress's death.

He also alleged to have knowledge of a red leather-bound diary that Monroe kept. Grandison stated in Slatzer's 1992 book *The Marilyn Files* that this diary contained scandalous information Monroe had assembled about the Kennedys, Monroe's friend Frank Sinatra, members of organized crime such as mobster Sam Giancana, and others. Among the alleged information was proof that the Kennedys had contracted with underworld figures in a failed plot to kill Cuban leader Fidel Castro. After Monroe's death, Grandison claimed, someone stole the diary from a safe in the coroner's office.

A private investigator named Milo Speriglio, meanwhile, claimed that he had proof of secret tape recordings that Monroe made of her conversations with both John and Robert Kennedy. These tapes were so scandalous that they would easily have toppled the Kennedy administration. Speriglio made his allegations in a 1975 article by Anthony Scaduto, "Who Killed Marilyn Monroe?" Speriglio told Scaduto: "Marilyn knew more about what the President was doing, thinking, planning, than the public, the press, the Congress, the Senate, the Cabinet and even the Attorney General."

Later, Speriglio and Scaduto changed their story. Expanding his story into a book called *Who Killed Marilyn?* and using the pseudonym Tony Sciacca, Scaduto claimed the tapes were not made by Monroe. Instead, the source of the tapes was alleged to be a wiretap specialist named Bernard Spindel, whose clients included the infamous labor union boss Jimmy Hoffa.

According to Speriglio and Scaduto, Hoffa hired Spindel to collect embarrassing information on Robert Kennedy, who was then conducting a vigorous campaign to put Hoffa in prison for a variety of racketeering (organized crime) offenses. However, Spindel's story seems questionable at best. At the time he came forward with his story, the wiretap expert was also facing imprisonment on charges of illegal wiretapping. It seems likely that he created the story in an attempt to strike a deal with authorities. In any event, no tapes were ever brought forward or used by Hoffa to sidetrack Kennedy's investigation, which eventually put Hoffa behind bars.

Anthony Scaduto charged union president Jimmy Hoffa (pictured) with gathering dirt on President Kennedy, including his affair with Marilyn Monroe.

Later, in his 1982 book *Marilyn Monroe: Murder Cover-Up*, private eye Speriglio said he interviewed someone who had once worked for Spindel. This former employee, who has since died and is identified only as Tom, claimed he heard a tape recording of a phone call made to Monroe's house from someone in San Francisco on the night of her death, asking, "Is she dead yet?" Tom also said he heard a recording made in the Monroe house on which there are sounds of Monroe being beaten, followed by a man's voice asking, "What do we do with the body now?"

Besides his allegations of wiretapping and secret tape recordings, Speriglio also mentioned a number of other theories about Monroe's death that he believed were worthy of consideration. These notions, none of which is backed up by evidence, include the following: (1) that Monroe died at Peter Lawford's house and that Lawford and Robert Kennedy took her body in a car back to her house; (2) that Monroe died at the Cal-Neva Lodge in Lake Tahoe and that her body was flown to Santa Monica Airport and driven by car to her home; and (3) that she died in a different part of her house, following a violent struggle, and was then carried back to the bedroom.

Tracking Robert Kennedy

In his book Legend: The Life and Death of Marilyn Monroe, *Fred Guiles reported that the FBI was very interested in Robert Kennedy's movements during Monroe's final days.*

"In the wake of Marilyn's death, FBI director Hoover asked for a complete rundown on Bobby Kennedy's movements during the weekend she died. Hoover received a three-page summary of Bobby's weekend activities beginning with his flight from Washington early Friday afternoon. According to this document, Bobby changed planes in Chicago, where he joined Ethel and four of his children for the flight on to San Francisco. Upon their arrival, the Kennedys were met by their weekend hosts, Mr. and Mrs. John Bates. This document reveals nothing of Kennedy's movements during the weekend, not until his return from [the Bates ranch at] Gilroy, California, to San Francisco on Sunday night. Hoover was reported to have learned further details of Kennedy's weekend from his friend, gossip columnist Walter Winchell."

In Double Cross, *ghostwritten for the brother of underworld gangster Sam Giancana (pictured), the author implicates Giancana in Monroe's death.*

The Mob and the FBI

The same rumors that link Monroe's death with the Kennedys also tend to include organized crime figures. One such story appears in a book entitled *Double Cross*, ghostwritten by an unnamed writer for the godson and brother of Sam Giancana. Giancana was a friend of Frank Sinatra's and a leading figure in the Chicago underworld. Various stories over the years make him either the sworn enemy of or the secret friend of the Kennedys; the former because Robert Kennedy was waging war on organized crime, the latter because the Kennedys were allegedly arranging for the gangster to secretly perform undercover work for them.

According to the colorful scenario in *Double Cross*, Giancana ordered a pair of men named Needles and Mugsy to travel from Chicago to Los Angeles on the weekend of Monroe's death. The two men waited patiently on the street while Robert Kennedy engaged in a final lovers' quarrel with Monroe. They then broke into her home and gave her a fatal barbiturate suppository. The idea, according to the book, was either to make it look like Monroe committed suicide over her broken affair with RFK or to frame him for the murder. Either way, Kennedy would have been ruined.

Other theories have emerged postulating that the FBI—and in particular its legendary first director, J. Edgar Hoover—was involved in Monroe's death. The fiercely conservative Hoover had an obsessive hatred of the Kennedys, particularly Robert Kennedy. He apparently kept extensive files on the brothers in order to maintain a fund of potentially embarrassing information. For instance, when Hoover learned that Capell's book (the first public accusation of an affair between RFK and Monroe) was about to be published, he sent a gleeful note to Robert Kennedy to inform him that the book would, if necessary, be used against him. Kennedy ignored the allegations.

According to Summers, the FBI confiscated Monroe's telephone records shortly after her death. These records allegedly contained proof that Monroe spoke with Robert Kennedy shortly before her death—an action he consistently denied. Summers quoted as evidence the testimony of a man identified as a close friend of the (since deceased) division manager for the General Telephone

J. Edgar Hoover (left) with Robert Kennedy. One theory implicates FBI director Hoover in Monroe's death.

Murdered

Robert Slatzer, who claims to have briefly been married to Monroe, is firmly convinced that Robert Kennedy ordered her murder. In his book The Life and Curious Death of Marilyn Monroe, *he writes:*

"According to what I have learned, RFK's sworn deposition [allegedly made in secret to the L.A. Police Department] detailed his visit to Marilyn's house that Saturday afternoon. This would at least verify some of the information I've gathered. Moreover, from my source comes a sensational revelation of what we may expect to learn from Bobby Kennedy's statement to the police. My information is that RFK admitted he'd gotten a call at Peter Lawford's house early Saturday afternoon. Marilyn was on the other end. She was in a state of hysteria and demanded to see him. He went to her house with a doctor and found her in a rage. She lunged at Bobby, trying to claw him, and he apparently had to knock her down. Then, as Bobby held her struggling body, the doctor injected what was probably a tranquilizer under her left armpit."

company: "He [the division manager] told me that the FBI came in and got the records, the next day."

Summers wrote that he also found a former FBI agent who in 1962 was in charge of organized crime investigations in "a major West Coast city." This man told Summers, "I am convinced that the FBI did remove certain Monroe phone records. . . . It had to be on the instruction of somebody high up, higher even than Hoover." The agent implied that orders from "higher even than Hoover" could only have been from the president or the attorney general. Summers theorized that Hoover helped the Kennedys obtain and suppress these potentially damaging documents in order to place the brothers in his debt.

All the people who knew firsthand the truth about what happened that night—including Ralph Greenson, Eunice Murray, Robert Kennedy, and, of course, Monroe herself—are dead. The endless digging into what did or did not happen in the house on Fifth Helena will no doubt continue for years to come. In the meantime, Monroe's legend—the person she was and the work she did—burns bright.

The Goddess

This will be a small funeral so she can go to her final resting place in the quiet she always sought.

Joe DiMaggio to reporters at Monroe's funeral

Permit me to express a faint hope that Marilyn Monroe be allowed to rest in peace.

Los Angeles District Attorney John Van de Kamp, concluding his 1982 reopening of the case

In the days following Monroe's death, a grieving Joe DiMaggio made the arrangements for her funeral. Monroe's mother was confined to a home for the mentally ill, her half-sister was unable to cope, her other friends and associates were too stunned or too embarrassed to take charge. Once more, Joe DiMaggio came to Monroe's rescue when no one else would.

Late in the afternoon of Monday, August 6, DiMaggio arranged for Monroe's body to be brought to Westwood Village Mortuary, a small cemetery near her home. Years before, she had asked Allan (Whitey) Snyder, her favorite makeup artist, to make sure she looked good at her funeral. On Tuesday Snyder arrived at the mortuary to perform his sad task and found DiMaggio sitting beside Monroe's body. On Wednesday Snyder came back, knowing that his final makeup job for Monroe would need retouching. DiMaggio was still there; he had stayed with her all night.

DiMaggio insisted that the funeral be small and intimate. The hundreds of photographers and reporters who showed up were kept outside the walls of the mortuary. People who DiMaggio felt had wronged Monroe—the Hollywood crowd that he disliked so much, including Frank Sinatra, Dean Martin, and the Lawfords—were turned away. Only thirty relatives and close friends, including

Grief-stricken Joe DiMaggio wept at Marilyn's funeral, bending over her casket and whispering, "I love you."

Greenson, Murray, and Monroe's acting coach Lee Strasberg, were allowed in. Arthur Miller did not attend; nor did any representatives of the Kennedy family.

Monroe was buried in a stylish green Pucci dress that she especially liked. At the service Lee Strasberg and a local minister delivered short speeches. The minister took his sermon from the Book of Amos: "How wonderfully she was made by her Creator." Just before the casket was closed, a weeping DiMaggio bent over to kiss Monroe and place a bouquet of pink roses in her hands. For the next twenty years, he would send flowers to her burial site weekly, just as he had promised on their wedding day many years before. DiMaggio has never spoken Monroe's name to a reporter again, has never remarried, and has always maintained a dignified public silence about his former wife.

The Legend Lives On

Amid all the gossip about celebrity, the legend that has grown up around her, and the endless speculation about her death, it is easy to lose sight of Marilyn Monroe as a human being. She was a confused and confusing bundle of contradictions. She had intensely

Killed by Communists?

In this excerpt from Marilyn: A Biography, *Norman Mailer comments on the theory suggested by* The Strange Death of Marilyn Monroe, *a book written shortly after her death by a right-wing communist-hunter, Frank A. Capell.*

"Its thesis is that Marilyn was murdered . . . by a Communist conspiracy of agents expressly because she had threatened Bobby Kennedy with exposure. The corollary is that the Attorney General was secretly, even publicly, sympathetic (in 1962!) to left-wing groups. According to Capell, Dr. Greenson and Mrs. Murray were fellow travelers [communists], and Dr. Engelberg had been a member of the Party. It is, of course, a considerable metamorphosis to go from being a man or a woman with left-wing attachments to an agent capable of a job of murder for the more advanced echelons of the Soviet secret police—which is exactly the surrealistic apocalypse to which Capell's thesis leads—but his short book is nonetheless valuable [because he] gives a full if unconscious portrait of how sinister a figure Bobby Kennedy must have appeared to ultra-conservative groups. On reflection, that may serve to bolster [my] own argument that there was much motive for the right wing of the FBI or the CIA to implicate Bobby Kennedy in a scandal."

strong ambition and a mania for perfectionism in her work, but she was also insecure, confused, sloppy in her personal habits, and emotionally needy. She was adored by millions, but she never found lasting love or a stable relationship.

Her beautiful body made her famous, but she abused it by becoming addicted to prescription drugs. She was the ultimate sex symbol, but she yearned for the everyday pleasures of motherhood. Her greatest successes were comedies, but she longed to be taken seriously as a great dramatic actress. And though she tried to become one of Hollywood's first female independent producers, she remained trapped within the film industry's restrictions.

This puzzling, complex person became a legendary figure and the center of a great mystery. And yet she came from extremely humble beginnings. Few who knew Marilyn Monroe early in her life would have guessed that one day the world would find her endlessly fascinating.

While the controversy about her death is fascinating, at the same time it is important to remember who Marilyn Monroe was when she was alive. She was a flawed woman and a gifted actress who became an emblem of glamour and beauty for millions of people around the world. Standards of beauty change over time; in today's world of ultra-thin supermodels, she might be seen as too full-bodied or voluptuous to be considered a great beauty. Nevertheless, the best of her films—*Some Like It Hot, Gentlemen Prefer*

Her glamour and beauty keep Marilyn a Hollywood legend, though her life was marred by endless self-doubt.

Blondes, Niagara, Bus Stop, The Seven-Year Itch, The Misfits—have become classics that are still a pleasure to watch.

It is also important to consider what Monroe might have achieved if she had not been born in her particular time and place. Things might have been very different for her, for instance, if she and her doctors had better understood the long-term effects of barbiturate use. Many people today struggle with drug addiction, of course, but techniques for dealing with the problem are far more sophisticated and effective than they were in Monroe's time.

Things might also have been very different if Monroe had not grown up in the era before feminism. She might have been better able, for instance, to use her celebrity status to form the creative production company she had long dreamed of, thus freeing her from a studio that forced her to make inferior films. And she may have had a happier, more fulfilling life if any of the unfortunate circumstances in her childhood or adulthood had been different; if she had grown up less racked by self-doubt and insecurity, her life might have been radically different.

Meanwhile, more than thirty years after her death, the *Washington Post* ran an article on the phenomenal endurance of her fame headlined "Marilyn: Hits Like a Bombshell." Some seventeen plays have been written about her, including one by her former husband Arthur Miller and another by Norman Mailer. Several novels, over a dozen made-for-TV movies, and an opera have also been produced—not to mention the books and films featuring Monroe-like characters. A number of countries, including the United States,

Too Sweet

In this excerpt from their book Mondo Marilyn, *writers Richard Peabody and Linda Ebersole reflect on Monroe's mystique.*

"She was the epitome of sex in the repressed, uptight fifties, a harbinger of things to come. Looking up at her image, . . . she seems tame, almost demure. In today's culture, she would probably not be a big star. She would be too heavy, too soft spoken, too sweet, but she might just be your best friend."

Many countries, including the United States, have used Marilyn's picture on postage stamps, a lasting tribute to her fame and popularity.

have issued stamps in her honor. Contemporary singers like Elton John and Madonna have paid homage to her, either in their music or in their performances.

All her life, Marilyn Monroe loved mystery and intrigue. In the end, mystery and intrigue helped make her perhaps the most legendary woman of the twentieth century. And a legend, more than anything, is what she wanted to be.

Works Consulted

Peter Harry Brown and Patte B. Barham, *Marilyn: The Last Take.* New York: Dutton, 1992. A book allegedly detailing Monroe's last days. Full of imagined dialogue and questionable facts and assertions.

Frank A. Capell, *The Strange Death of Marilyn Monroe.* Zarephath, NJ: Herald of Freedom Press, 1964. By a right-wing researcher who saw Monroe's death as part of a vast communist conspiracy.

Ralph Greenson, "Special Problems in Psychotherapy with the Rich and Famous." Unpublished essay dated August 18, 1978. Part of Greenson's papers in the Special Collections Department, at the UCLA Library.

Fred Lawrence Guiles, *Legend: The Life and Death of Marilyn Monroe.* New York: Stein and Day, 1984. A book by a writer who concludes that Monroe committed suicide.

Ann Lloyd, *Marilyn: A Hollywood Life.* New York: Mallard Press, 1989. A collection of photos, many familiar from other sources, with short captions and quotes about Monroe.

Norman Mailer, *Marilyn: A Biography.* New York: Grosset & Dunlap, 1972. Not a biography at all, but a long essay in Mailer's windy, heavy-handed style. The accompanying photos are wonderful.

Richard Peabody and Linda Ebersole, eds., *Mondo Marilyn.* New York: St. Martin's Press, 1995. A collection of fiction and poetry about Monroe.

Anthony Scaduto, "Who Killed Marilyn Monroe?" *Oui* magazine, October 1975. The adult-magazine article that first speculated on the existence of Monroe's diary.

Robert F. Slatzer, *The Life and Curious Death of Marilyn Monroe.* New York: Pinnacle, 1974. By a man who claims to have been Monroe's friend, lover, and husband.

———, *The Marilyn Files.* New York: S.P.I. Books, 1992. A second volume by Slatzer.

Andrew Solt, director, *Remembering Marilyn.* Vestron Video, 1989. Documentary video featuring brief interviews and film clips about Monroe. A highlight is footage from her famous appearance at John F. Kennedy's birthday party.

Milo Speriglio, *Marilyn Monroe: Murder Cover-Up.* Van Nuys, CA: Seville Publishing, 1982. By a private investigator who claims to have uncovered proof of a murder and conspiracy.

——, *The Marilyn Conspiracy.* New York: Pocket Books, 1986. A rehashing of the author's alleged proof of murder.

Donald Spoto, *Marilyn Monroe: The Biography.* New York: HarperCollins, 1993. The fullest, fairest, and best biography of Monroe to date.

Anthony Summers, *Goddess: The Secret Lives of Marilyn Monroe.* New York: Macmillan, 1985. By a British writer who has also written books on the Kennedy assassination and J. Edgar Hoover.

Index

hospitalization of, 21
interest in Democratic politics, 71
John F. Kennedy and, 72, 78
marriage to
Arthur Miller, 16, 20
Jim Dougherty, 10, 12
Joe DiMaggio, 13, 14
modeling career of, 11–12
move to New York, 14–15
red diary of, 78
Robert F. Kennedy and, 52
as part of communist conspiracy, 73–75
rumors of affair between, 72–75
suffers miscarriage, 16
Mortensen, Norma Jean. *See* Monroe, Marilyn
Murphy, Eunice, 54
Murray, Eunice, 21, 23, 25, 37, 49
overdose and, 66
testimony of, 28–29
discrepancies in, 29, 68–70

Nembutal, 64
interaction with chloral hydrate, 65
levels in Monroe's blood, 39
Newcomb, Pat, 21, 25, 34, 37
New York *Herald Tribune*, 54
Niagara, 77
Noguchi, Thomas, 39, 51, 60
suspicions of cover-up, 56, 63

Olivier, Sir Laurence, 16
organized crime, 81

Parker, William
possible participation in cover-up, 42, 55
Peabody, Richard, 88
Playboy magazine, 13

Roberts, Ralph, 21, 72
Rudin, Milton, 28, 34

Scaduto, Anthony, 78
Schaefer, Walt, 31
Schenck, Joseph, 13
Sciacca, Tony, 79
Simpson, Keith, 51, 58–60
Sinatra, Frank, 24, 78, 81
Slatzer, Robert, 32, 77
on possibility of injected overdose, 60–61, 83
Smith, Jean, 74
Snyder, Allan (Whitey), 15, 84
Some Like It Hot, 18–19
Something's Got to Give, 22, 43
Spindel, Bernard, 79
Spoto, Donald, 17, 21, 44, 46, 61
on conspiracy rumors, 50, 72, 75
on overdose, 63–66
Stephens, Boyd, 53–54
Strasberg, Lee, 14, 85
Strasberg, Susan, 23
Summers, Anthony, 33, 38, 47, 51, 52, 56, 58, 72
on FBI, 82
on Monroe-Kennedy affair, 74
on Monroe's drug use, 54
on Monroe's suicide, 68

Tabachnick, Norman, 52
20th Century-Fox, 12

Van de Kamp, John, 71

Wallach, Eli, 19
Washington Post, 88
Who Killed Marilyn (Sciacca), 79
Wilder, Billy, 18
Winchell, Walter, 75, 80

Picture Credits

About the Author

Adam Woog is the author of several books for young people and adults. For Lucent Books, he has written *The United Nations, Poltergeists, The Importance of Harry Houdini, The Importance of Louis Armstrong, The Importance of Duke Ellington, The Importance of Elvis Presley,* and *The Mysterious Death of Amelia Earhart.* He lives in Seattle, Washington, with his wife and daughter.